T0208217

BE EXTRAORDINARY!

Devotions for Ordinary People Who
Want to Live Extraordinary Lives

YVETTE M. JONES

WESTBOW
PRESS®
A DIVISION OF THOMAS NELSON
& ZONDERVAN

WestBow Press books may be ordered through booksellers or by contacting:

WestBow Press
A Division of Thomas Nelson & Zondervan
1663 Liberty Drive
Bloomington, IN 47403
www.westbowpress.com
1 (866) 928-1240

ISBN: 978-1-9736-5867-2 (sc)
ISBN: 978-1-9736-5866-5 (e)

Library of Congress Control Number: 2019904050

Print information available on the last page.

WestBow Press rev. date: 04/25/2019

To my beloved family and friends, thank you for the role you played in my spiritual growth. Because of you I have endeavored to live an extraordinary life for Christ Jesus, my Lord and Savior. I pray you find the inspiration to do the same as you read this book.

May God give you a passion to be extraordinary for Him alone.

Thank You!

CONTENTS

EMBRACE THE POWER

"... casting all your anxiety upon Him, for He cares for you." I Peter 5:7

When emotions run high and thoughts flood your mind with symptoms of fear and doubt, know that the enemy is seeking a prey to poison and blind with His venom of negativism. *"The god of this world has blinded the minds of the unbelievers to keep them from seeing the light of the gospel ..."* (II Cor. 4:4). We are exhorted by the Apostle Paul to *"resist the devil ..."* so that He will *"... flee ..."* from us after we draw near to God with a submitted heart (James 4:7). We have the power to resist the devil in the Holy Spirit. *"We have this treasure in clay jars so that it may be made clear that this extraordinary power belongs to God and does not come from us"* (II Cor. 4:7).

Embrace the Holy Spirit's power in you and walk in victory today by taking every negative emotion and thought captive to the obedience of Christ. Make your emotions and thoughts line up with the Word of God and possess the peace that passes all understanding. Be anxious about no-thing and pray about every-thing that causes you to suffer anxiety (Phil. 4:4). Humble yourself under God's mighty hand by standing firm in faith and believe that He is able to handle what troubles and worries you. Leave your cares with Him and resist taking them back. If you worry about the same thing over and over and allow it to steal your peace, you have taken your anxieties back from the Lord. Learn to leave what burdens you to the only One who can carry them. Learn self-control and be alert, because the devil is constantly prowling and seeking to destroy the peace and joy of those who believe in Jesus. You have the power of Jesus to resist the devil—use it!—and let the peace of God rule in your heart today.

THE WINNING LOVE

"Love never fails." I Corinthians 13:8

"A new commandment I give to you, that you love one another; as I have loved you, ..." John 13:34

"He who has My commandments and keeps them, it is He who loves Me. And He who loves Me will be loved by My Father, and I will love Him and manifest Myself to Him." "If anyone loves Me, He will keep My word; and My Father will love Him, and We will come to Him and make Our home with Him." John 14:21, 23

How many times have we sung love songs to the Lord, not realizing that we are called to love Him through loving others? He places minimal value on words filled with love and devotion because they hold no value if we are not acting them out toward others. This is what Jesus had to say about sweet talk of love and devotion: *"These people draw near to me with their mouth, And honor me with their lips, But their heart is far from me. And in vain they worship me, teaching as doctrines the commandments of men"* (Matt. 15:8-9). Talk is cheap if there is no action behind it. How often have you heard phone conversations close with "I love you"? I have been the recipient of such word love from family members who have never done anything to demonstrate the love they expressed. Therefore, their words were received as empty cliché or slang. The commandments of men, meaning this society's norms, are to spread love words to all who you feel good about for the moment or for some personal advantage, but let that person offend you with words or disagree with your words and the love will vanish like vapor. We are so quickly offended with each other over words that we forget about the charge Jesus gave to love one another as a demonstration to the world that love lives in us. It saddens and grieves the Holy Spirit when love is not evident in the lives of God's people who are engaged in conflict. Paul exhorted us to overcome evil with good (Rom. 12:21). What is better than the winning kind of love that looks beyond the surface faults of others to their needs to be loved? Remember, we are called to be merciful, as God is merciful (Luke 6:36). This is a form of loving God's way— forgiving the offenses of others by refusing to keep records of them. There is a reason not to listen to everything people say about you, because you may fall prey to being easily offended. Take hold of the wisdom of Solomon and treasure these words: *"For there is not a just man on earth who does good And does not sin. Also, do not take to heart everything people say, Lest you hear your servant cursing you. For many times, also, your own heart has known That even you have cursed others"* (Ecc. 7:20-22). No one can take pride in not offending others with their words. We all have said things that we wished we could take back before it did any damage to the recipient. So, just as we want to be loved by others, we should love by not keeping a record of wrongs, but by overcoming every offense with winning love, a love that is not based on conditions or performance. The winning love is not a payment kind of love, expecting something in return, but is freely given because it was freely given by Jesus Christ: *"Beloved, if God so loved us, we also ought to love one another. By this we know that we abide in Him, and He in us, because He has given us His Spirit. But the fruit of the Spirit is love, ..."* (I John

4:11, 13; Gal. 5:22). Go and tackle today with a winning love! Demonstrate real love, the love of God, to a world that needs love more than words. "… *let us not love in word or in tongue, but in deed and in truth*" (I John 3:18).

HIDDEN BEAUTY

"You are the light of the world. A city that is set on a hill cannot be hidden. Nor do they light a lamp and put it under a basket, ... Let your light shine before men, ... and glorify your Father in Heaven." Matt. 5:14-16

What are you hiding under? Why are you not allowing the beauty of what God created in you to shine and beautify this ugly world? God gave us His light so we can light up the darkness in this world, not hide from it. If we don't shine what God has given us, we are hiding it under something. A revelation came to me the day I took off my wig and discovered the beautiful hair I had been hiding for several years. Because I didn't realize the beauty of the hair God gave me, I hid it under wigs and weaves for more years than I want to count. I was under the mindset that beauty was in the fake hair because it was the latest fad. Now I am free to let the light of day shine on my real hair and enjoy the freedom of letting my hair down. I am grateful to God for this revelation and the hair that He took the time to count every strand of to show He knows what is best for me. You may not be hiding a full head of hair under a wig, but maybe you are hiding under work-a-holism and find yourself too busy to smell the roses or enjoy the people in your life. Maybe you are hiding in front of the TV or in the shopping mall. Just know, *"No one after lighting a lamp hides it under a jar or puts it under a bed, but puts it on a lamp stand, so that those who enter may see the light. For nothing is hidden that will not be disclosed, nor anything secret that will not become known and come to the light"* (Luke 8:16-17). It's foolish to think that we can hide what God has created to be seen. No matter what your hiding object or place is, it is time to let your light shine, so that others may glorify God, the Father in you.

FAVOR!!!

"For You, O LORD, will bless the righteous; With favor You will surround Him as with a shield."
Psalm 5:12

We are blessed with a favor that moves mountains, opens doors that no man can shut, makes ways when there is no way, gives wings to fly when weights of the world press hard upon you, a favor that defends you before adversaries, and makes your dreams come true. This favor is God's favor shining upon you in the mirror of grace through the Lord Jesus Christ. If Jesus did not lay down His life for us, we would not have God's favor. Do you live like you have favor with God? One way to tell is to evaluate whether your faith is producing extraordinary favor in your life. Is your life a reflection of a victor or a victim? Do you live like God is your Father and the source of all your needs or do you live by chance, and accept whatever comes your way? The truth and Good News is that you have the favor of God available to you for every valley experience you face in life. But you have to exercise your faith to activate and receive God's favor in order to climb the next mountain. You must believe what the Apostle Paul said, *"But without faith it is impossible to please Him, for He who comes to God must believe that He is, and that He is a rewarder of those who diligently seek Him"* (Hebrews 11:6). Another truth in James reveals how important faith is in receiving from God, *"But let Him ask in faith, with no doubting, for He who doubts is like a wave of the sea driven and tossed by the wind. For let not that man suppose that He will receive anything from the Lord; He is a double-minded man, unstable in all His ways"* (James 1:6-8). Wow! No faith ignited, no favor received. I remember the time when we were selling our 1975 MGB sports car and many inquiries came, but no buyer. I realized that doubtful fear was hindering us, so I sought the Lord to deliver me from my fears. The word of the Lord that gave me a breakthrough said, *"Without a vision, the people perish"* (Proverbs 29:18 KJV); *"Where there is no revelation, the people cast off restraint; but happy is He who keeps the law"* (Proverbs 29:18 MacArthur Study Bible). It was time to pray for a vision of a buyer coming to buy the car with cash in their hand. It was difficult at first to capture a vision or revelation that God was going to reward me with a buyer, but the power of the Word of God granted the desire of my heart. I began to thank God daily for the buyer who had money in hand to purchase our car. To my surprise, exactly what I believed I received. I saw the reality of my vision come to fruition as the buyer drove off in our car. Faith in God's almighty power and standing on His Word is the pathway to living an extraordinary life, one that defies reasoning and rational thinking. Faith moves mountains, parts seas, stops issues of blood, feeds thousands, opens blind eyes and deaf ears, heals the lame, and puts money in the mouths of fish.

This truth freed me to re-evaluate whether my faith was producing the results of a victorious life. Once I grabbed ahold of this truth and recognized what belonged to me, God's favor, I rose off the bed of a defeated and discouraged mentality and shook myself to get in line with God's Word. Live like a woman highly favored of God. See His favor in every area of your life, even your health, wealth, weight struggles, and dreams. As the angel told Mary, *"Do not be afraid, Mary, for you have found favor with God"* (Luke 1:30). I like the King James translation that says, "highly favored by God." Embrace God's favor today and begin to live the extraordinary life you and I were created to live, a life filled with faith-filled expectancy. Someone once said that our lives are the result of what we have settled for. Do not settle for less than God's best in every area of your life.

THANK-FULL

"Enter into His gates with thanksgiving, …" Psalm 100:4

"O, that men would give thanks to the Lord for His goodness, …" Psalm 107:8

"Let them sacrifice the sacrifices of thanksgiving, …" Psalm 107:22

Today, we have the opportunity to fill our mouths with thanksgiving to the Lord instead of requests. Start off your day by thanking Him for waking you up; keeping you safe throughout the night; providing a bed and bedding, a home for shelter; and for allowing you to walk, see, hear, and speak. There are so many things to thank the Lord for in every new day. Miracles happen when you give the Lord thanks. Jesus demonstrated that when He gave thanks for the two fish and five loaves of bread that fed the five thousand, leaving twelve baskets of leftovers (John 6:5-13). If you need a miracle today, try thanking the Lord for what He has already given you—enough to perform a miracle. To feed five thousand with two fish and five loaves of bread seemed ridiculous and impossible, but it was enough for the Lord because little is much when we place it in the Master's hand. Give Him your little with thanksgiving and see what He will do. There is power in praising the Lord with a thankful heart, because it allows you to fill your innermost being with gratitude that often leaks out through holes created by complaining. When we fail to give thanks for what we have and acknowledge that it is enough, we limit the power of God from moving on our behalf. You think you don't have enough money, time, love, peace, rest, friends, or possessions because the world and all its marketing devices tell you that something is missing and deprived in your life. Their advertisements poke holes in your heart and fill you with discontentment and the feeling that there is always something lacking in your life. But when you read the Bible, especially the Psalms, you will find many exhortations directing you to give thanks for the good things the Lord has already done for you. The Apostle Paul said, *"in everything give thanks; for this is the will of God in Christ Jesus for you"* (I Thess. 5:18). The Lord is waiting for you and me to bless Him with praises of thanksgiving for all He has done for us up to today. Fill yourself up with thanksgiving to the Lord so you can experience His miraculous power in your life and your cup will overflow with thanksgiving so that you will become Thank-full.

WHAT IS YOUR TRUE TREASURE?

"For where your treasure is, there your heart will be also." Matthew 6:21

What dominates your time and uses up your energy? Are you on a quest to get as much of the American Dream as you can so you can lay back, take it easy, and someday retire? Or, are you spending yourself for others to be enriched? Beware of the seduction of the American Dream to accumulate stuff for self, like houses, fine cars and clothes, exotic vacations, and multiple luxuries. Listen to the warning signs, *"Do not store up for yourselves treasures on earth, ... But store up for yourselves treasures in heaven, ..."* (Matthew 6:19-20 NIV). If your mind is filled with thoughts about your needs only, then you will treasure and worship self. But if you are always thinking of ways to improve the lives of others, then you will treasure giving and serving others. I remember the story of the rich man, who daily enjoyed the best things in life: expensive clothes and feasts, while continuously ignoring the cries of a poor sick man named Lazarus who begged for crumbs enough to satisfy His hunger. The rich man had worked to lay up treasure for Himself, which clearly reveals where His heart was focused, on himself. Another warning against living to satisfy only self, *"... Be on your guard against all kinds of greed; life does not consist in an abundance of possessions"* (Luke 12:15 NIV). *"... God knows your hearts; for what is prized by human beings is an abomination in the sight of God"* (Luke 16:15 NRSV). The Apostle Paul clarified whom we should treasure and live for, *"He died for all, so that*

those who live might live no longer for themselves, but for Him ..."
(II Cor. 5:15 NIV). The bottom line is this: strive to become rich toward God by seeking the things of His kingdom, to store up in your heart things that are of high value and profitable. Store up His Word in your heart and you will know the difference between living for self and living to serve others as you serve Him. *"Agree with God and be at peace; thereby good will come to you. Receive instruction from His mouth, and lay up His words in your heart. ... if you lay gold in the dust, ... then the Almighty will be your gold and your precious silver"* (Your treasured possessions). *"For then you will delight yourself in the Almighty ..."* (Job 22:21-26 ESV). Treasure the things God treasures. Treasure the things the world treasures and you will know that your heart does not belong to God, but to this world, and that you have devoted yourself to the things it values and treasures—stuff. *"Do not love the world or the things in the world. If anyone loves the world, the love of the Father is not in Him"* (I John 2:15 ESV).

MOVING ONWARD!

The Lord said to Moses, "Why do you cry to Me? Tell the people of Israel to go forward." Exodus 14:15 ESV

"To everything there is a season, a time for every purpose under heaven." Eccl. 3:1 Berean Study Bible

What season are you stuck in? Is there a stagnated area in your life where the waters of life are not moving? Are you so nostalgic that you cannot break free of the past? It is evident that some people do not grow up and move away from symbols and idols that have been long gone. For example, idols like Marilyn Monroe, Elvis Presley, James Dean, and Michael Jackson continue to be worshipped by millions of followers— some even dress and act like them. Letting go of what has died and passed away is hard for many, especially when their identities are tied up in them. But life was created to be lived in daily newness because each day is a new day. There is a time to let die those things that hold you back from becoming what God created you to become. Everyone will eventually lose something of deep significance and value. Loved ones, friends, and others you have idolized should never keep you from moving forward, nor should you live for them by imitating them. You must be you and embrace your own identity because, as the psalmist said, you were fearfully and wonderfully made by God (Ps. 139:14). You must be uniquely you in order to move onward. I like what the Apostle Paul wrote about letting go of the past: "… *one thing I do, forgetting those things which are behind and reaching forward to those things which are ahead, I press toward the goal for the prize …*" (Phil 3:13-14). Are you pursuing any goals or dreams? What drives you to move from where you are to where you want to be, or are you stuck? If you are stuck (like in a snowstorm), you don't have to stay stuck, you can free yourself by choosing to embrace the newness of life that has been gifted to you today and walk in it. Jesus encourages His followers not to look back or mentally live in the past when He said, "*No one, having put His hand to the plow, and looking back, is fit for the kingdom of God*" (Luke 9:62 NKJV). You cannot move forward while looking back, for you will surely stumble and get stuck in a rut. Ever try to drive forward looking only in the rear-view mirror? If you did not look in front of you, you would get in an accident and probably end your life. Start today anew and live in the presence by being present. Choose to embrace the gift of life God has bestowed on you, for it is to be used for living. Tell yourself every day to "move onward" if you feel that something is trying to hold you back and stick you to yesterday. Whenever discouragement, despair, or depression confronted me, I told myself the following statements: "This is only for a season." "This too shall pass." "Every moment that is passed is gone forever." Try one of these on yourself and get moving into what you were created for today.

A CONSISTENT LOVE

"Because your steadfast love is better than life, my lips will praise you." Psalms 63:3 ESV

Why do we run around trying to find love? We look for it from our families, friends and others, but often find ourselves with a greater craving to be loved. We try to manipulate and entice others into loving us, only to find that their love vanishes like smoke in the sky. We think we would be loved if we looked a certain way, wore a certain style of clothing or hair-do (wigs, extensions, weaves, perms), worked in a high-profile position, drove a certain car, lived in an exclusive neighborhood, vacationed at exotic places, or possessed many objects of wealth. The commercials and mass advertisements today promote products with the promise that you will love yourself after purchasing their products. Diet ads promote the testimonies of users who give tearful claims that they finally love themselves, now that the weight is off. This world is thirsty for love. Could it be that we are looking for love in the wrong places, from all the wrong sources? Even people in the church do not realize that God is love, and that He has already proven His love for mankind through Jesus' death on the cross at Calvary. *"For God so loved the world, that He gave His only Son, so that whoever believes in Him should not perish but have eternal life"* (John 3:16 ESV). This famous verse has been memorized and quoted by many for thousands of years, but many still starve to be loved. I believe God loved us so we would not perish without love. *"See what kind of love the Father has given us, that we should*

17

be called children of God; …" (I John 3:1). We are already loved, and that love was displayed over two thousand years ago. *"God's love was revealed among us in this way: God sent His one and only Son into the world so that we might live through Him"* (I John 4:9 Christian Study Bible). *"… if we love one another, God abides in us and His love is perfected in us. … So, we have come to know and to believe the love God has for us. God is love, and whoever abides in love abides in God, and God in Him"* (I John 4:12, 16). Reading these passages leads me to believe that in order to believe I am loved with a steadfast and unfailing love; I must freely give away what I received. Having God's love is better than life to me because His love never fails. He is always with me when family and friends abandon me. I can trust and count on Him to be always present even when I don't see signs of His presence. He has proved His love for me in many ways, like forgiving me when I mess up, healing me when sickness attacks my body, strengthening me when I am weak, giving me guidance when I don't know the way to go, and providing patience when I want to hurry and become anxious about so many things like Martha. Tears fill my eyes when I think of how the Lord has loved me with His very life. I was blind to His love, even as a Christian, but His Word opened up my understanding of His steadfast and unconditional love. I have grieved many times after foolishly looking past Him for love. I found a love that endures forever, and I want to remind you of how much you are loved. Stop looking for love from family and friends. True love is only a breath away. All you have to do is call on the Lord of love and He will pour His love into your heart. Know and believe that He loved you with His life when He laid it down for you at the Cross of Calvary. Settle the manner of love and declare you are loved by love Himself. *"Once God has spoken; twice have I heard this: that power belongs to God, and that to you, O Lord"* (Psalms 62:11-12). Begin to declare today: *God loves you just the way you are.* You don't have to lose the weight for Him to love you, you don't have to dress in designer fashions, you don't have to be rich, you don't have to have a high profile job, you don't have to wear the latest hairstyle or expensive jewels, all you have to do is believe in God's love. I did, and it continues to change and renew my warped way of thinking about love. The truth of God's love has freed me to love with a love that never changes, a consistent love that is not performance based, but unconditional. Embrace the truth about real love today and walk in love. Declare you are loved when your feelings say the opposite.

STAND!!!

"Therefore, take up the whole armor of God, that you may be able to withstand in the evil day and having done all to stand; Stand therefore, having girded your waist with truth, having put on the breastplate of righteousness, and having shod your feet with the preparation of the gospel of peace; above all, taking the shield of faith with which you will be able to quench all the fiery darts of the wicked one." Eph. 6:13

When floods, storms, and other trials come upon you, stand firm, trusting in the armor the Lord has covered you with—Himself. He is the truth around your waist, the breastplate of righteousness that protects your heart, the peace that you walk in, the shield of faith to extinguish the enemy's fiery darts and daggers, the helmet of salvation that assures you of God's saving grace, and the sword of the Spirit that brings the Word of God to your mind. You have been covered with the full armor of God for each day's battles, but know that the armor is rendered inactive if your total trust is not in the Lord to activate it and fight for you. All the Lord is asking of you and me is to stand still and fix our eyes on Him, the author and finisher of our faith. You must respond to adversity with the stance and stately stride of a lion who does not turn away or retreat before anything, but moves with a stately bearing (Prov. 30:29). Look adversity in the eye with a footing that cannot be threatened or moved by fear. Fix the eyes of your heart firmly on the truth, believing that the Lord will never leave you nor abandon you during times of trouble. Speak the words of the Psalmist, *"God is our refuge and strength, an ever-present help in trouble. Therefore, we will not fear though the earth gives way and the mountains fall into the sea, though the waters roar and foam and the mountains quake with their surging"* (Ps. 46:1-3). Stand when it seems like everything around you is shaking, flooding, surging up, and falling apart. You choose to stand in faith or fall in fear. The choice is yours. If you choose to put yourself in a position of faith without wavering in unbelief, but giving glory to God, you will see that the Lord performs what He promised (Rom. 4:20-21). Stand no matter what you feel, even if your aging body is weak, stand firm on the promises of God and you will see His mighty power displayed. If your faith weakens, gain strength through reading and meditating on the historical facts in the Word of God when He commanded His people to take a position and stand until they saw Him save them from that which pursued them to harm and destroy. As Moses said to the children of Israel, I say to you, *"Do not be afraid. Stand still and see the salvation [deliverance] of the Lord, which He will accomplish for you today ... The Lord will fight for you and you shall hold your peace"* (Exod. 14:13-14). There will be a season and time in your life when you must be quiet (still) and wait upon the Lord. He wants you to know that He will glorify His name in your life. Be still and stand, knowing that He is God and that He will not share His glory with any other source of deliverance that is at your disposal. No one will get the credit for making a way out for you, only God gets the glory. Stand quiet and wait on the Lord, be of a good courage in the waiting. Do what David said, *"Be still and know that I am God"* (Ps. 46:10). Do what the prophet Isaiah said, *"In returning and rest you shall be saved; in quietness and confidence shall be your strength*" (Isa. 30:15). So, after you have done all you can do to move forward into the things the Lord created you for, and nothing seems to progress, stand still and quietly wait with your heart firmly positioned in the faith that what the Lord promised you He is able to perform. Embrace the "quiet phase" of the new thing the Lord is doing in your life to enable you to move forward into a new chapter, a new campaign in which He will raise the awareness of His presence in your life. He will take you into the public phase, where He will get the glory for moving you into what He created you for.

Take Up Your Position Of Faith!

"Watch, stand fast in the faith, be brave, be strong."
I Cor. 16:13 NKJV

"Be on your guard; stand firm in the faith; be men of courage; be strong" (I Cor. 16:13 NIV)

Every day is a new day, a day that has never existed before, a day of new choices and new opportunities. We all begin our days making choices, whether good or bad. You choose to get out of bed, wash your face, brush your teeth, shower, and clothe yourself. You choose what and when to eat; you choose whether to exercise your spirit toward godliness by having a devotional time, or run to the gym to exercise your body. You choose to think positively or negatively about the day you have been given, but regardless of what you have chosen, the day is full of choices. The point I want to challenge you with is this: Will you chose fear and discouragement over faith and courage? What you decide will frame the kind of day you will have. You may have a day filled with challenging trials, emotional struggles, or physical barriers, but you do not have to allow these things to change your position of faith and push you into the dungeon of fear. The Apostle Paul exhorted us in the above scripture to *"Watch, stand fast in the faith."* He knew that circumstances and events can knock us off our feet and cause us to become afraid, fearful, and discouraged. But if you remember to seek the Lord first for help throughout the day, and cast all your anxieties on Him, you will not have to fight for your position of faith. Have faith in the Lord who can uphold you throughout the day and keep you from falling into fear and discouragement. Truly cast all your cares on Him and let Him care for you. He will carry you when you become too weak to stand; for when you become weak, the power of Christ will have the opportunity to rest upon you. Just remember that the battles of the day belong to the Lord when you seek and trust Him. All you have to do is what the prophet Jahaziel said to King Jehoshaphat, *"Do not be afraid or discouraged because of this vast army. For the battle is not yours, but God's ... You will not have to fight this battle. Take up your positions, stand firm, and see the deliverance the Lord will give you. Do not be afraid; do not be discouraged"* (II Chron. 20:14-17). Every day has its own battles, but you can choose to turn them over to the Lord and let Him fight them for you. He is a mightier warrior than you. Just take your position and stand firm in the faith you have in Him to work all things out for your good and to finish the work He has begun in you (Romans 8:28). Your days are in His hands and He will perform all the things that concern you if you seek Him and trust Him with all your heart (Jer. 29:13). Refuse to lean on your own understanding (Prov. 3:5). Finish the day with giving Him thanks for His love for you.

WHAT NOT TO DO WHEN SUFFERING

"Before Him no creature is hidden, but all are naked and laid bare to the eyes of the One to whom we must render an account." Hebrews 4:13

There are times in our lives when we feel all alone in our sufferings and that no one really cares about our pains. You feel like your prayers are bouncing off the ceiling and coming back unanswered. You begin to think that God have abandoned you and turned a deaf ear to your petitions. Everything around you suggests that you are all alone in the burden of your pains. But can this physical evidence be reliable and trusted? No! Because we all know how unreliable feelings are and how quickly they can change. The truth is that God's eyes never leave you. He who keeps watch over you never slumbers or sleeps. If you don't feel Him near, maybe it's because He is carrying you. Hear what Isaiah the Prophet said, and be encouraged, *"Why do you say … my way is hidden form the Lord and my right is disregarded by my God? Have you not known? Have you not heard? The Lord is the everlasting God, the Creator of the ends of the earth. He does not faint or grow weary … He gives power to the faint and strengthens the powerless. Even youths will faint and be weary, and the young will fall exhausted; but those who wait for the Lord shall renew their strength, they shall mount up with wings like eagles, they shall run and not be weary, they shall walk and not faint"* (Isaiah 40:27-31).

You are never alone! God is with you always! *"Do not fear! For I am with you, do not be afraid for I am your God; I will strengthen you, I will help you, I will uphold you with my victorious right hand"* (Isaiah 41:10).

Take charge of your feelings and align with what God says. Begin to declare His continual presence in your life by speaking the truth to your surroundings and say, *"God is with me. He promised never to leave me even in times of suffering. He is my help in times of troubles."* Recite the words of King David and encourage yourself, *"God is our refuge and strength, a very present help in trouble"* (Psalms 46:1). Do not settle for thoughts that say, "The Lord has forsaken me, and the Lord has forgotten me." Remember, *"Can a woman forget her nursing child and not have compassion … surely they may forget, Yet I will not forget you. See, I have inscribed you on the palm of My hands"* (Isaiah 49:14-16). Although many are the afflictions of the righteous, the Lord will deliver them when they wait and endure until He shows up.

IS ANYTHING TOO HARD FOR THE LORD?

"*Ah, Lord God! Behold, You have made the heavens and the earth by Your great power and outstretched arm. There is nothing too hard for You.*" Jeremiah 32:17

"*Behold, I am the Lord, the God of all flesh. Is there anything too hard for Me?*" Jeremiah. 32:27

What are you struggling to believe the Lord for? Is it the salvation of a loved one? Is it healing of a sickness or disease? Is it finding a job? Is it direction for the future? Are you having a hard time believing that the Lord is guiding you in the way you should go because you don't see any directional signs? We all at one time or another struggle in our faith and find it difficult to see beyond present circumstances, especially those trials that attack our faith. But hold on to your faith without becoming faint and weary in the well doing of believing in the Lord to perform the impossible. Do not let your current predicament and problems steal your belief in the Lord. Remember the circumstances in Jeremiah's day. The Lord told Him to purchase land that was going to be destroyed and wiped out, not fit for anyone to live on. A land destroyed by the enemies of the Lord's people. Jeremiah could not see beyond the current predicament of His people, nor beyond God's inevitable judgment. Even though His prayers sounded good and contained faith-filled words, the Lord knew He had some questions about how the Lord was going to restore and revive that which had been devastated. Take to heart and think about the Lord's reply to Jeremiah, *"Behold, I am the Lord, the God of all flesh. Is there anything too hard for Me?"* (Jer. 32:27). In essence, the Lord was telling Jeremiah that as He allowed destruction to happen to His people, so could He restore and revive what had been destroyed. Even what seems unsellable because of its condition, the Lord can make sellable. The Lord said to Jeremiah, *"Just as I have brought all this great calamity on this people, so I will bring on all the good that I have promised them."* If the Lord promised you anything, He will perform it, because He is not a man who lies. What is impossible for men is possible with God. He is not limited by current predictions of doom for the economy, nor moved by the housing market crisis, the unemployment rate, or racial inequality. He is not even limited by your thinking or doubting thoughts. He is almighty and powerful and absolutely nothing is too hard for Him. I know, because He has shown me many signs and wonders of His great power.

For example, I was barren, unable to conceive and He opened my womb and blessed me with not one, but two children. I was filled with so much fear of rejection and abandonment and He healed me with an abundance of love poured out by His Spirit into my life. I have seen His power displayed in foreign lands as well as in America throughout my world travels. I am fully persuaded that what the Lord promised you and I, He is well able to accomplish. There is nothing too hard for Him if you believe in His great and mighty power, for His arms are not too short that He cannot reach down and touch your life. He has a mighty, outstretched arm waiting for you to put your trust in only Him. ♥

BANISH FEAR!!!

"Do not fear, for I am with you, do not be afraid, for I am your God; I will strengthen you, I will help you, I will uphold you with my victorious right hand." Isaiah 41:10

Have you ever wondered where all the fear we feel and think comes from? Is there any justification for most of our fears? Do we have the right to be afraid of the unknown, of what people may do to us or what storms will come upon us? Searching for answers from the scriptures, I can find no justification for the fears that have tormented me over the years. The fear of people, the fear of being raped, the fear of harm coming to my family, the fear of cancer or heart attack, the fear of want, the fear of inadequacy, the fear of failure, the fear of losing a job, the fear of persecution, the fear of losing love, the fear of being cheated on, the fear of abandonment, the fear of accidents, the fear of being disabled, and many others, have creeped into my mind like a thick fog that makes it hard to see clearly. Fear distracts and blinds you from seeing the Son through the fog and fixing your eyes on the truth that Jesus is still with you. You have to get sick and tired of living in constant torment, of going from one fear to another, and begin to banish each fear-filled thought before it comes to fruition and produce what you really don't want. Just know that fear loves to activate your faith in it and steal it from God. This happened to the disciples when they were in a boat with Jesus and quickly forgot who was with them and that He cared about them. The disciples woke Him and said to Him, *"Teacher, don't you care if we drown?"* He said to His disciples, *"Why are you so afraid? Do you still have no faith?"* (Mark 4:40). Storms will come, fog will come, wind will blow, floodwaters will rise, terrorists will strike, jobs will be lost, some will die from cancer and others from sickness and disease, disabilities will limit mobility, feelings of inadequacy will come, but know that the Lord is still on the throne. He is faithful to His promise to be with you in the midst of the storms of life if you put your faith in Him and not into what you fear. Faith is the key to banish fear from your life. Learn to fight fear at the first sight of it in your mind by using the weapons God has given you. *"For the weapons of our warfare are not merely human, but they have divine power to destroy strongholds* [fear is a stronghold of Satan]. *We destroy arguments and every proud obstacle [fear is an obstacle that blinds] raised up against the knowledge of God, and we take every thought captive to obey Christ"* (II Cor. 10:4-5). In order to operate from the mind of Christ, faith must be fixed upon Jesus Christ, the author and finisher of our faith. *"For we walk by faith, not by sight"* (II Cor. 5:7). *"For God did not give us a spirit of fear* [cowardice, timidity] *but a spirit of power, of love and of a sound mind"* [self-discipline] (II Timothy 1:7). We have been given power from on high to banish all fear from our lives that does not agree with what God says is ours. Remember, *"There is no fear in love, but perfect love casts* [banishes] *out fear; for fear has to do with torment* [punishment], *and whoever fears has not reached perfection in love"* (I John 4:18). The bottom line is, if you really love the Lord, you will not fear anything or anyone. When fear comes to catch you off guard, immediately fix your eyes on the presence of the Lord and cling to Him, like a magnet to a refrigerator, until the fear-filled thoughts pass. If you resist fear and banish it from your mind, it will flee from you and you will enjoy the liberty that comes from the Spirit of the Lord. *"Now the Lord is the Spirit, and where the Spirit of the Lord is, there is freedom"* [liberty] (II Cor. 3:17).

A Safe Place

"He who dwells in the secret place of the Most High shall abide under the shadow of the Almighty ... Because you made the Lord, who is my refuge, even the Most High, your dwelling place, no evil shall befall you nor shall any plague come near your dwelling." Psalm 91:1, 9-10

Where do your run for shelter and protection when the storms of life bring feelings of jeopardy? Who do you talk to about the concerns of your heart? Who can you rely on? Who is your confidante? Who has your back when things seem against you? Who can you be yourself with and pour out your heart to in honesty and truth? Who knows you better than anyone else? Whose friendship will never abandon you? Who will never leave you, nor forsake you, nor let you beg for bread? Who carries you through life when you are too weak to stand or walk? Whose love is enough to fill your life with contentment? These are just a few questions that have confronted me during my journey as I searched the Word and my heart for answers. I have learned by listening to the Holy Spirit that the Lord provides the safest place for me to run to when my world feels like it is falling apart. I find my safe place in His presence—the place of prayer, the quiet place in which I meet with Him. He is the only One who knows me better than my husband, children, and friends. He knows how much I can handle and when the loads of life weigh me down. I can also pour out my heart and tell Him about all my struggles and insecurities and leave His presence with an assurance that He is able to accomplish the work He began in my life and bring it to completion. I don't have to wallow in self-pity or low self-esteem, because the Lord said He would be my confidence as I put my mind on Him. There is not a need in my life that He is unable to meet. People have failed me. Family and friends have abandoned me, but the Lord has been a friend who has stuck closer than a brother. He adopted me when my father and mother forsook me. He placed me in a family when I wandered the streets of cities alone, hungry and hopeless, by creating a family for a hopeless, homeless, and helpless barren woman. He has been the calm in all my storms. His words of encouragement have lifted my head and heart so many times that I can believe that my dreams can come true because the dream-maker is on my side. He has protected me in the midst of snowstorms and whiteouts and brought me to safety. All that I have needed to become the wife, mother, grandmother, and homemaker I am today has been provided by my heavenly Father and God. I cannot think of a safer place to run to than the arms of the Savior. He is Almighty and will do amazing things for you if you would just give Him all the controls of your life. Let go and let Jesus be the Lord over your life. He wants to be your safe place. Storms will come, people will disappoint, family and friends will abandon and forsake you; confidants will betray your secrets, but the Lord will never leave nor forsake you. He gives His angels charge over you to keep you in all your ways. ♥

Just Wait!

"Wait for the Lord; be strong and let your heart take courage; wait for the Lord!" Psalm 27:14

In our society, we are constantly bombarded with a spirit of urgency and speed. We get impatient and angry when someone slows us up. Look at some of the ways we have been seduced by this spirit of urgency: we want our food fast, we want to travel in the fast lane without anyone in front of us, we want our appointments to be on time with minimum waiting, we want our family members to move to our drumbeat, we want to get rich quick, and we want to lose weight with the swallow of a pill or a drink that promises fast results. What's the hurry? What's going on? Why all the panic? I believe all this pushing to live life in the fast lane is making us incapable of waiting. The more we adopt the habit of doing everything in a hurry, the less appealing and acceptable waiting is in our lives. Why do our highway signs have so many warnings about slowing down to save lives? Even in the church today, the spirit of urgency is causing people to look at their watches if the sermon goes long. The main point I want to make is that all this rushing around is hindering our relationships with the Lord. You can't hurry the Lord to answer your prayers, to give you what you want, to heal your body, or to open up a door of opportunity or ministry. He knows you will be tempted to be impatient and discouraged by the delays, this is why He repeatedly says in His Word to wait on His timing. I learned that waiting involves being strong and courageous. The temptation to become weak and discouraged is the strongest during these times. If we expect to receive anything from the Lord, we must learn to wait and see. Listen to what the Lord said to Joshua when He took the leadership role that Moses had held, *"Have I not commanded you? Be strong and courageous; Do not be terrified, do not be discouraged, for the Lord your God will be with you wherever you go"* (Joshua 1:9). *"Wait for the Lord and keep His way"* (Psalm 37:34). Be still before the Lord and wait patiently for Him ... Commit your way [waiting] to the Lord; trust in Him and He will do this ... (Psalm 37:5-7). Whatever it is you want from the Lord, it must be received according to the Lord's timetable, not yours. Since you know our society is obsessed with hurrying, why not retrain yourself to slow down and wait. Practice on the things in your life that you are prone to do in a hurry. Maybe waiting on someone else by slowing down your pace in the supermarket or on the highway. If you use the words "Hurry, let's get moving." "Move it fast." "I'm in a hurry, could you speed it up, please?" Begin to remove these action words from your vocabulary. Just know that God wants to bless you with an abundant life, but you have to slow down in order to enjoy the little things you already have. Take time to play with your children or assemble a puzzle with your spouse. Most of the things you think have to be done right away. Stop and smell the roses. Stop pulling, pushing, and rushing your children through stores as if you're competing in a race. Learn the art of sitting quietly in prayer and meditation before the Lord. Resist the temptation to honk at drivers in front of you who wait too long for the light to change. Waiting an additional second may be what saves you from an accident. *"Be still and know that I am God"* (Psalms 46:10). Do not be in a hurry to leave the King's presence (Ecclesiastes 8:3). Learn to pray and wait. *"In quietness and trust is your strength ... Blessed are all who wait for Him"* (Isaiah 30:15-18). ♥

HEART TROUBLED

"Let not your heart be troubled; you believe in God, believe also in Me ... Believe Me that I am in the Father and the Father in Me, or else believe Me for the sake of the works themselves ... Let not your heart be troubled, neither be afraid." John 14:1, 11, 27

Does your heart feel like a troubled sea that is churning and casting up all the mire and dirt of your life to choke out your peace? Do troubling thoughts keep flooding the shores of your mind and drown out any hope of having peace of heart and mind? The present and future seem to offer no hope of overcoming a troubled heart that has been infected by the negativity of this world. News programs like CNN love to broadcast breaking news of evil tidings that bring great sorrow to its viewers. You can't find any hope or Good News watching today's news shows. What is going on? Why are there so many troubled hearts in this world? Is there a battle against peace? Why isn't the church praying for peace to rule in the hearts of God's people around the world, that their hearts would not be troubled by the cares and troubles of this life? Perhaps it is because their hearts are too troubled and heavy laden with fear and their prayers have been buried under the mire and dirt of this world. But if you are reading this devotion today, you can impact this present day by redeeming the times and preparing the way for the Lord's return. All you have to do is hear the truth about what is really going on. There is a spiritual battle fighting against our Prince of Peace. The battle starts in your mind when you embrace the fear of man and let it penetrate your heart, causing unrest and uncertainty. Hear what the Lord God said through the prophet Isaiah, *"of whom have you been afraid or feared that you have lied and not remembered Me, nor taken it to your heart? I, even I, am He who comforts you. Who are you that you should be afraid of a man who will die and of the son of a man who will be made like grass? And you forget the Lord your Maker ... and have feared continually every day ... Listen to Me you who know righteousness, you people in whose heart is My law: Do not fear the reproach of men nor be afraid of their insults"* (Isa. 57:11; 51:7, 12-13). A society of troubled hearts is nothing to be alarmed about. Jesus said that in the last days, men's hearts will fail them because of fear, but you must not let fear trouble your heart. Embrace the truth of God's Word and remember how He kept you over the years, months, and days. He has been your shield and hiding place and has given you Himself to keep you calm. Let Jesus Christ live big in you today and impact this world of troubled hearts for Him by not allowing the thief of peace rob you of what is rightfully yours, the peace of God that is beyond understanding. He is able to calm the troubled sea in your heart and bring you to still and restful waters. Live in peace today. ♥

WHERE IS YOUR FAITH?

"Do you believe that I am able to do this? According to your faith let it be done to you." Matthew 9:28-29

Jesus asked this question of the two blind men who sought Him for restoration of their sight. *"Do you believe I am able to do this?"* He was asking if they believed He was able to restore their sight. They replied, *"Yes, Lord,"* and their sight was restored. Many times, I have read this passage and believed Jesus was asking me the same question when I sought Him for my needs. I know this passage wasn't written for me, but it was written for me to find the will of the Lord for my life. As the blind men sought to heal their blindness, I sought the Lord for mercy to forgive my sins and received healing of spiritual blindness. It is by faith that blindness is healed, and hemorrhages were dried up in a woman who suffered bleeding for twelve years. Faith in Jesus brings down the power of God and something happens immediately—a miracle is birthed. Hear what Jesus said to the woman who believed that if she touched His cloak she would be made well, *"Take heart daughter; your faith has made you well. And instantly the woman was made well"* (Matthew 9:22). Faith is the key that unlocks and releases power from Heaven. You can't receive anything from the Lord if you don't believe He is able to do what you need. Jesus emphasized the importance of faith when He told a leader, *"Do not fear, only believe ..."* (Luke 8:50). Fear will steal your faith for itself and produce negative results, that which you do not want. As Joel Osteen said about faith and fear, "they have something in common.

Both ask us to believe something that we cannot see" ("It's Your Time," p. 94). Why waste your faith believing what fear says you see and feel, when you can receive what you thought was impossible? Why not be the one that Jesus refers to when He said, *"Someone touched me for I noticed that power had gone out of me"* (Luke 8:46). Remember the following truths and receive what you expect: *"Without faith it is impossible to please God, for whoever would approach Him must believe that He exists and that He rewards those who seek Him"* (Hebrews 11:6). You must seek only God as the source of all your needs. *"Now faith is being sure of what we hope for and certain of what we do not see"* (Hebrews 11:1 NIV). You must be fully persuaded and certain that God will come through for you. *"This is the confidence we have in approaching God: that if we ask anything according to His will, He hears us. And if we know that He hears us—whatever we ask—we know that we have what we asked of Him"* (I John 5:14-15 NIV). Live in confidence today and touch Jesus for yourself so that His power may be released into your life. Live believing and not fearing. God is the only One who can produce a miracle in your life. Adopt the attitude of Abraham and declare, *"No distrust made Him waver concerning the promise of God, but He grew strong in faith as He gave glory to God, being fully convinced that God was able to do what He had promised"* (Romans 4:20-21). *"For nothing will be impossible with God"* (Luke 1:37). Who is your faith in? Are you seeking the Lord our God as the source for what you need? I sought the Lord when the elders in my family said I would never conceive children due to damage done to me by a rapist when I was only five years old. I sought God's healing of my barren womb and put faith in His promise that He causes barren women to conceive. In time, I became a joyful mother of two daughters (Psalm 113:9). Though God does not always answer our prayers as we would like, believe that He

Yvette M. Jones

is able to perform the impossible in your life. Either way, you will be blessed and may find a new desire in your heart. Touch Jesus today and believe He is able. Seek Jesus to heal you from blindness to the truths that can free you to live by faith today and tomorrow. *"For we walk by faith, not by sight"* (II Cor. 5:7).

PERFECT PEACE

"You will keep Him [her] *in perfect peace whose mind is stayed on You, Because He* [she] *trusts in You."* Isaiah 26:3

Why does it seem like the battles in your minds never seem to end? You wake up every morning confronted with bombarding thoughts of whether to listen to the feelings of your flesh that often try to get you to embrace the negative. You are naturally prone to follow your feelings and allow them to dictate the kind of day you will have: A day of defeat, sickness, depression, or discouragement. You have to choose before you act on these thoughts. "I don't want to get out of bed. I think I will stay in bed all day," "I feel like I am coming down with something," "I don't feel too good about myself," or "No one cares." All of these mind battles are tricks of the enemy, the devil, who is trying to trick you and steal your inner peace. You have to shake yourself free and come to your senses daily and clothe yourself with the truth. What does the Lord say to you about the things that seem to bring you down and steal your peace? I have found these truths that I hope will free you to make this a great day, one in which you walk in the freedom that Christ died to give you. The prophet Isaiah said, *"You will keep him in perfect peace Whose mind is stayed on You, because he trusts in You"* (Isaiah 26:3). The Apostle Paul said that Jesus is our peace: *"He Himself is our peace"* (Eph. 2:14). He also exhorted the believer to think on things above, those things that are true, noble, just, pure, lovely, of good report, virtuous, and praiseworthy (Philippians 4:8). But remember not to be anxious about anything and pray about everything, then the peace of God that surpasses all understanding will keep your heart and mind through Christ Jesus (Phil. 4:6-7). When Jesus told the disciples not to let their hearts be troubled by fear of abandonment when He left them to return to the Father, He told them that He would leave them His peace: *"Peace I leave with you, My peace I give you; not as the world gives to you. Let not your heart be troubled, neither let it be afraid"* (John 14:27). Jesus is that perfect peace that is beyond our understanding. He will manifest His presence in your life when you put your total reliance on Him when the raging seas of your mind come in on you like a flood to swallow up your inner peace. Embrace the truth and cast down the lies of the devil that seek to bring you down and trouble your heart. Know that the Comforter has come, and He abides in you because Jesus did not leave you without a Comforter, but sent the Holy Spirit in His place: *"when He, the Spirit of truth, has come, He will guide you into all truth"* (John 16:13). What truths do you need to fix your mind on today to make it a great day? Try the truth that the Holy Spirit lives in you and that His fruit—love, joy, and peace (Gal. 5:22), is at your disposal. Let the Holy Spirit control your mind and think on what He brings back to your remembrance, whether it was through the prophets of old or the Apostles, it is still the word of the Lord. So, choose perfect peace by keeping your mind fixed on the promises of God and the devil will take a hike once He sees that you will not allow Him to rob you of the truth.

ENOUGH SLEEPING! TIME TO AWAKEN

"Awake, awake, put on strength, O Zion!" Isaiah 52:1

"Are you asleep? Could you not keep awake one hour? Keep awake and pray that you may not come into the time of trial." Mark 14:37-38

According to Ecclesiastes 3:1, *"There is a time for everything, and a season for every activity under heaven"* (NIV). I believe this includes a time to sleep and a time to wake even though they are specifically mentioned in Ecclesiastes 3. The church has slept long enough and taken its rest instead of staying awake and praying for the will of the Lord. Trials and temptations are flooding into this world in alarming proportion, seducing many away from the faith and to the lust of the flesh, the lust of the eyes, and the pride of life. The church is filled with prosperity messages more than messages on fasting and prayer, watching and praying, and living holy, for God's will to be done, not ours. We have allowed the devil to rock us to sleep in our pursuit for provisions and power. The way the church looks on the surface, with its sumptuous living and feasting, it is evident that the church loves what the world offers: fine clothes, cars, and luxurious lifestyles. The devil has tempted the church to want what the kingdoms of the world offer more than what the kingdom of God offers. *"The devil took Him to a very high mountain and showed Him all the kingdoms of the world and their splendor and He said to Him, 'All these things I will give you, if you will bow down and worship me'"* (Matt. 4:8 NIV). Has the church fallen into the temptation of worshipping the devil? Has the church fallen to sleep on the truths about living for the kingdom of God? What is the church devoted to? The church's devotion is revealed in the messages that are preached. We were warned by John not to love this world or the things in this world because these things steal our devotion to God. *"The love of the Father is not in those who love the world—the desire of the flesh, the desire of the eyes, the pride in riches—comes not from the Father, but from the world"* (I John 2:15-16). Jesus gave many similar warnings when He said, *"No one can serve two masters, either He will hate the one and love the other, or He will be devoted to the one and despise the other. You cannot serve both God and money* [wealth]" (Matt. 6:24). There is so much worship of wealth going on in the church today that my heart cries because I, too, have been rocked to sleep by the comfort of these things the world offers to make one's life better. Yet, is life better when you are asleep to the truth and don't know it?! Many have fallen away from the faith in the state of slumber as they have been driven to pursue the splendors of wealth. *"People who want to get rich fall into temptation and a trap and into many foolish and harmful desires that plunge men into ruin and destruction ... Some people eager for money have wandered from the faith and pierced themselves with many griefs* (I Tim. 6:9-10). We are given many warnings to prevent us from falling asleep on the truth. Times of testing in what we love and seek will come to all who profess Christ. They will either live through His power or deny His power by having a form of godliness to fool those around them (II Timothy 3:1-5). The Apostle Paul said, *"Find out what pleases the Lord"* (Eph. 5:10 NIV). Therefore, it says, *"Sleeper, Awake! Rise from the dead and Christ will shine on you. Be careful then how you live, not as unwise people but as wise, making the most of the time, because the days are evil. So, do not be foolish, but understand what the will of the Lord is"* (Eph. 5:10, 14-17). It is time to return to watching and praying for the things that break the Lord's heart, that souls are lost and need to be found, time to seek the Kingdom of God to come on earth through our lives, it is time to wake up from our laziness and rise up from our sleep. If we don't wake up, poverty will come. *"A little sleep, a little slumber. A little folding of the hands to rest and poverty will come up you like a robber and want [desires] like an armed warrior"* (Proverbs 24:33-34). Do whatever you need to do to wake up to God's call to watch and pray. If you have to remove some of those things you have idolized and accumulated, things that have taken a lot of your energy (mental and physical) and time, get rid of them. The things of this world only clutter our lives and weigh us down with anxiety. Refuse to fall sleep any longer on the Lord. Shake yourself and stand up for the Lord. *"Awake, awake, put on your strength, O arm of the Lord ... awake, awake! Stand up!"*

FEAR OF NOT BEING LOVED

"Praise the Lord, For His mercy endures forever."
II Chron. 20:21

"… I have loved you with an everlasting love. …"
Jer. 31:3

There is so much fear permeating our society today that it is no wonder Christians struggle with the love question. The fear of being unappreciated is associated with the fear of not being loved because the two are connected. People shorten their lives seeking escape from a society in which true love seems unattainable. When I was a child, it was unbearable to accept a life without being loved by those closest to me, so I resorted to methods that would shorten my suffering and end my pain, but thanks to God, I did not succeed. Suicide is not the answer, nor option to escape a loveless society or family. There is a better way to overcome the battle against this destructive fear, which is found at the feet of Jesus Christ. He demonstrated God's love for all humanity on Calvary's Cross when He willingly took on our sins, paying the price of great suffering to bring us under God's love. The truth is we do not have to be afraid of not being loved anymore because God has richly lavished His love on us through Jesus Christ. You are loved regardless of what you feel during emotional meltdowns. You are loved regardless of what you hear about in these times in which we see so much hate demonstrated. You are loved in spite of the number of calls or acts of love you receive from others. If no one loves you back for all the love you have showed them, you are still loved with the everlasting love of God. During times of struggle, when fear of not being loved bombards your mind, encourage yourself with God's Word by speaking it over your life. Say, "I am loved! Nothing can separate me from God's love. Jesus loved me with His life. I am covered in love because God's banner over me is love. Everywhere I turn, there flies high the banner of love. How could I doubt His love when He demonstrated it by sacrificing His only begotten Son to die that I may be loved? I am loved, and the gates of hell cannot prevail against God's love for me." Saying such affirmations to yourself will lift you up and free you from the devil's schemes to steal, kill, and destroy you through fear. Remember, the devil is the father of lies—lying is His profession. It is a lie that you are not loved. When the power of negative suggestion floods your mind during times of weakness, stand firm on the truth of God's Word and declare in the face of the enemy that you are loved and nothing he can do can separate you from the love of God that is in Christ Jesus. ♥

WHOM SHALL I SEND, WHO WILL GO FOR US?

"How are they to hear without someone to proclaim Him? How are they to proclaim Him unless they are sent?" Romans 10:14-15

What is the divine commission for you? Do you know what the Lord has called you to do? Can you hear Him calling your name? Do you see the directional signs He has given you to instruct and teach you in the way you should go? Why are you standing still? Why are you settling on the mountains of familiarity and letting your understanding limit you? Why are you building settlements as if this place is your home? Perhaps you have lost sight of God's purpose and plan for your life. He has placed a calling on all our lives and that calling is the divine commission, the mission He wants us to go on. Have you argued with God and given Him excuses for why you have not gone on the mission ordained by the Lord? Moses learned that excuses about abilities and what people may think or say mean nothing to the Lord, nor do they outweigh His mission. If He appoints a task to us, we must perform it without reservation, but in confidence that God knows what He is doing. He will equip you with whatever you need for a successful mission. *"Now go and I will be with your mouth and teach you what you are to speak,"* is what the Lord told Moses about His view about His communication skills (Exodus 4:12). The Lord is calling for messengers to proclaim His Good News to those bombarded with bad news. He wants to touch your mouth with live coals from heaven's altar to purify and prepare your mouth to be used for His glory. He wants to save your mouth and redeem your lips from speaking for yourself and the world. In the words He used to call Isaiah, He says to you and me, *"Whom shall I send and who will go for us?"* (Isaiah 6:8). What will your answer be? Will you say, "Here am I; send me?" Or will you flee from the presence of the Lord God, like Jonah, because your ego, credibility, and people's opinions mean more than turning people to the Good News of Jesus Christ? Is doing what you want in this life more important to you than doing the will of the Lord? *"Does not the potter have the right to make out of the same lump of clay some pottery for special purposes and some for common use?"* (Rom. 9:21 NIV). God made us for Himself that our lives may proclaim Christ, the Savior, to a world gone mad. *"We do not live to ourselves ... if we live, we live to the Lord ... we are the Lord's"* (Romans 14:7-8). He paid for us with His life's blood. *"You are not your own ... you were bought with a price; therefore, glorify God in your body"* (I Cor. 6:19-20). We don't have the option or right to do whatever we want or go wherever we want. We are commissioned soldiers for the Lord. *"Let each of you lead the life that the Lord has assigned to which God called you"* (I Cor. 7:17). So, when the Lord says to go speak to a person or group, give no excuses, just go, and know that He will give you the words. *"You shall go to all to whom I send you and you shall speak whatever I command you ... for I am with you. Then the Lord put out His hand and touched my mouth; and the Lord said, now I have put My words in your mouth, See, today I appoint you ..."* (Jer. 1:7-10). Know that if the Lord sends you on a mission, He has already equipped you with the necessary abilities to complete it. If He appoints you, He anoints you with His presence; therefore, you have nothing and no one to fear. Just be willing and obedient to the call of God upon your life and daily say, *"Here I am Lord, Send me!"*

LISTEN MORE THAN YOU TALK

"Everyone should be quick to listen and slow to speak." James 1:19

"Let your words be few." Eccl. 5:2

Who has your ear? Who is the one you give great attention to and whose words you do not want to miss? What or whom you listen to will determine whether your will end your day feeling defeated or victorious. If you listen to negativity, gossip, bad news, and complaints, you will finish the day feeling downcast and discouraged. But if you choose to listen to what the Lord says, you will close the day feeling hopeful and encouraged. His words edify and lift the soul into a sphere of freedom. Jesus said if we continue in His Word, we will know the truth and the truth will set us free (John 8:32). The only way to receive this freedom is to listen intently to what the Lord is saying and repeat it to yourself and to others as you would repeat the latest breaking news of a tragedy. It is time to take back control from the enemy of our souls and enter into the self-discipline of listening more and talking less. We have been given two ears and one mouth so as to listen twice as much and talk half as much, yet the opposite happens. In a society filled with multiple talk shows of people spilling their guts about everything that enters their minds, little discipline is evident. The scriptures make it clear that we should tame our tongues, lest we miss many a blessing from the Lord that comes from listening to Him. So why not begin today and train yourself to speak your peace less and listen more. You may hear the still small voice of the Lord instructing you on how to handle that problem you have been dealing with. You can do all things through Christ who strengthens you (Phil. 4:13). The Lord does not ask us to do what is impossible, but He provides the help needed to succeed. Can you hear what the Lord is saying today?

King David said, *"Blessed is the man who does not walk in the counsel of the wicked ... but delights in meditating in the law of the Lord"* (Psalm 1:1-2 NIV). Your blessings are dependent on what you listen to and believe. As you think, so you will become. If you think fearful thoughts, you will respond in fear-driven actions. If you hear a cracking sound in the house, you will get up and check the house, finding it was only the wind blowing. Fear can cause you to jump at every little sound. This is why it is vitally important that you pay close attention to what you listen to and evaluate what kind of spirit is behind the scene, whether the spirit of lies or the Holy Spirit of truth. The words you hear in your mind or through the mouth of others are spirits. Jesus made this point clear to the disciples when some decided to desert Him: *"The words I have spoken to you are spirit and life"* (John 6:63 ESV). So be careful today with what you listen to and make sure you are listening to counselors of faith and courage and not the wicked counselors of fear who have been hired by the devil to whisper words of fear and discouragement and sabotage your plans to rebuild your life around words that give life.

Start casting down every word you hear that does not uphold the words the Lord has spoken to you and choose to listen to: *"Fear not, for I am with you"* (Isaiah 41:10 ESV); *"Be strong and courageous"* (Joshua 1:6-9 ESV), *"... a very present help in trouble*" (Psalm 46:1b ESV); "*I can do all things through Him who strengthens me*" (Phil. 4:13 ESV); "*No weapon formed against you shall prosper ...*" (Isaiah 54:17a NKJV) because the battle is the Lord's.

WHAT YOU SAY IS WHAT YOU'LL GET

"I tell you the truth, if anyone says to this mountain, "Go throw yourself into the sea," and does not doubt in His heart but believes that what He says will happen, it will be done for Him. Therefore, I tell you, whatever you ask for in prayer, believe that you have received it, and it will be yours." Mark 11:23-24

What are you speaking into your life and the lives of your family and friends? Have you ever evaluated the source behind your words? Do you really want or believe some of the things you have said, "These children are driving me crazy!" "I am about to lose my mind!" "This work is killing me!" "I will kill you if you say that again!" "It is raining cats and dogs!" "This _____ is making me sick!" "I am frightened to death when I _____." "I am confused." "I just don't know." "Nobody cares." "Everyone takes advantage of me." "My hair is so thin." "I am afraid of _____." "My neighbors keep to themselves." "They are trying to fire me." "A conspiracy is forming against me." "My supervisor doesn't acknowledge my good at work, only my faults." "I'm afraid of losing my job." "I am afraid of dying from what my father and mother died of." "No one likes me." The list of things we say to ourselves and others that are based on lies is endless. A wise woman once told me that she did not permit all the thoughts that came into her mind to make a nest. It was apparent that she rejected the negative thoughts and held onto to the positive ones. She impressed me so that I started practicing screening my thoughts to see if they lined up with Philippians 4:8: *"Whatever is true, whatever is noble, whatever is right, whatever is pure, whatever is lovely, whatever is admirable, if anything is excellent or praiseworthy, think about such things."* This tells me that our words are formed by the thoughts we dwell on.

What are you meditating on these days? Are your thoughts filled with the promises of God or the problems of this world? You have the control to cast down whatever image or thought that does not agree with what God has promised you, so take charge and change what you don't like on the projection screen of your mind. Remember, there is power in your words because your words produce more of its kind. You produce death or life through your words. Are you killing yourself and murdering others? You are if you are speaking words that contain deadly venom that destroys love, joy, and hope. *"Death and life are in the power of the tongue, and those who love it will eat its fruit"* (Proverbs 18:21). Satisfy your life and your innermost being by speaking life to yourself and claiming what is yours in God, not what you feel, or see. *"From the fruit of the mouth one's stomach is satisfied; the yield of the lips brings satisfaction"* (Proverbs 18:20). Store up words in your mind and heart that yield good treasure, good fruit that feeds life into those around you. Jesus said, *"For out of the abundance of the heart the mouth speaks ... on the day of judgment you will have to give account for every careless word you utter; for by your words you will be justified and by your words you will be condemned"* (Matt. 12:34-37).

Start now and change your words. Begin speaking truth to yourself and others today, say what God says and you will resist the lying words of the enemy of your soul. Say, "I am more than a conqueror." "I can do all things through Christ." "God is causing me to triumph in Christ Jesus." "I am victorious." "I am healed." "I am strong." "I am free to love as I have been loved." "I forgive as I have been forgiven." "I am loved with a steadfast love." "His banner over me is love." "I am highly favored among women." "The favor of the Lord surrounds me as a shield." "The Lord is my strength." "I am never alone because the Lord is with me." "I am not afraid of man or woman, beast or foe, because God did not give me a spirit of fear. He gave me a spirit of power, love, and a sound, unconfused mind." "I am being guided because the Lord is my shepherd." "I lack no good thing, because surely goodness and mercy is following me all the days of my life." "No weapon formed against me will prosper." "In the name of the Lord, I will destroy my enemies."

COUNSELORS OF FEAR

"Do not believe every spirit, but test the spirits to see whether they are from God." I John 4:1 NIV

"Don't believe everything you hear. Carefully weigh and examine what people tell you." 1 John 4:1 The Message

The Word of God is clear about taking seriously what you listen to, knowing that counselors of fear are roaming around seeking to destroy someone's faith in God. Paul exhorted us to be sober and alert, because our adversary, the devil, is roaring and roaming throughout the earth for prey to seduce with His lies.

Everyone who speaks to us during times of trouble and trials does not always have our best interests at heart when their words are filled with discouragement and fear. Some have good intentions, but they often result in fear taking dominion over those who step out of the boat to walk on water with Jesus. Step out on your dreams by sharing with others what you believe God will do and someone will tell you a report of one who tried that and was destroyed by the giants. A good example of this is found in the book of Numbers when twelve spies searched a land filled with all they could ever need. Ten spies came back to camp with a bad report and two came motivated with faith and courage. The ten spies took on the role of counselors of fear when the children of Israel listened to what they said and became paralyzed by the fear of being destroyed by giants. Listening to the spirit behind the majority of spies caused many of the children of Israel to die with their dreams of entering a land flowing with milk and honey. Have you let counselors of fear steal your dream of doing or becoming what God has promised? Commit today to not letting that happen anymore. ♥

The Fragrance Of Love

"We are to God the aroma of Christ among those who are being saved and those who are perishing."
2 Cor. 2:15

"Since God so loved us, we ought to love one another."
I John 4:11

I love visiting gift shops filled with pleasant scents that make you feel warm and fuzzy, like sitting in a warm and cozy place in front of a fireplace on a cold winter's night beside the one you love. The beauty of some of these gift shops mimics country living with all the earth tones and smells that it makes it difficult to leave. I have often wondered how they make all the scents work together without creating a sickening smell. I leave these shops wishing I could duplicate the aromas in my home so that guests would feel at home. I wonder if my guests smell the fragrance of love through the things I have prepared to celebrate their visit? What aromas are filling the air from my greetings, words, and gestures? Reading various passages in the Bible has challenged me to evaluate what scents I am sending into the atmosphere of the people I interact with. Am I spreading the fragrance of God's love through living a life of love? If not, what am I spreading? Am I spreading the aroma of fault-finding, criticism, or negativism by always finding something wrong in my life or the lives of others? Living in a society that promotes the faults and wrongs in the lives of others is clothed in negativism. It is a daily challenge to think positively while turning on the fault-finding search light to find something wrong. But if you and I allow the Holy Spirit to counsel and guide us on how to live a life of love, our aroma can change from bitter to sweet and love can destroy records of wrongs we see in our lives. We ought to fill every atmosphere we enter with the fragrance of love, permeating the nostrils of those around us like the scents in the gift shops. People who come into contact with us should feel the warm and fuzzy feelings of love, not the human kind, but the love of God that penetrates our spirits. Ask yourself this, "What fragrances or scents am I spreading into the atmosphere around me?" "Do those who come into contact with me feel loved?" If we, those saved by God's grace, do not fill the atmosphere of this world with unconditional love, the world will not get to know God, because He is love. We are called to be God's priests with incense lamps swinging and filling the atmosphere with the fragrance of God's love. So let us live lives of love, intentionally seeking those who need to smell the sweet aroma of Jesus. ♥

THE CALL

---

*"The Lord called Samuel a third time and He got up
and went to Eli and said, 'Here I am, for you called
me.' Then Eli perceived that the Lord was calling the
boy ... if He calls you, you shall say, 'Speak, Lord,
for your servant is listening.'"* I Samuel 3:3-10

Although Samuel was raised by Eli, the prophet, to conduct
religious services in the temple of the Lord, He was not
familiar with the word of the Lord, nor did He know the
voice of the Lord. When He heard His name being called,
He thought it was Eli calling Him, but it was the Lord. The
Lord called Him four times before He answered. What was
the call? It was to be a mouthpiece (a spokesman) for the Lord
to speak what He says to whom He says, regardless of their
rank or position. How many times has the Lord called your
name? Have you mistaken His call for the call of someone else
by seeking the mission others wanted you to go on? Are you
fulfilling someone else's call for your service now? How many
more times does the Lord have to call your name before you
say, *"Here I am. Speak, Lord, for your servant is listening."* God is
looking for those who will make themselves available for His
service by coming to Him for instructions on fulfilling the call.
Jeremiah recognized that the calling of the Lord was on his life
from birth: *"'Before you were born I consecrated you; I appointed
you'* ... *"'Then I said, Ah, Lord God! Truly I do not know how to
speak'"* ... *But the Lord said, 'you shall go to all to whom I send you
and you shall speak whatever I command you'"* ... *"Then the Lord*

put out His hand and touched my mouth; and the Lord said to me, 'Now I have put my words in your mouth'" (Jer. 1:4-9). Excuses about limited abilities don't hold any weight with the Lord, nor is He moved with compassion when we give Him excuses of why we can't fulfill His call to serve on His behalf.

Jeremiah's excuse of being too young and inexperienced in speaking to nations or leaders did not move God nor change His plan and purpose for Jeremiah's life. Jeremiah was called to be a mouthpiece for the Lord regardless of His evaluation of his age and abilities. A similar situation happened when the Lord called Moses out of the burning bush. *"Then Moses said, 'I must turn aside and look at this great sight and see why the bush is not burned up.' When the Lord saw that He had turned aside to see, God called Him out of the bush, 'Moses, Moses ....' But Moses said to the Lord, 'O my Lord, I have never been eloquent, neither in the past nor even now that you have spoken to your servant; but I am slow of speech and slow of tongue.' Then the Lord said, 'Who gives speech to mortals? Now go, and I will be with your mouth and teach you what you are to speak.' But He said, 'O my Lord, please send someone else.' Then the anger of the Lord was kindled against Moses and He said, 'I will be with your mouth'"* (Exodus 3:1-4; 4:10-15). Moses tried to change God's calling on His life by giving more than one excuse about his lack of abilities, not realizing that whom God calls He equips and empowers. Fear is often behind the excuses we give the Lord when He calls us. We fear the unknown, we fear being embarrassed (suppose they do not believe me or listen to me), we fear our inadequacies, and we fear people. The Lord is looking for willingness and availability from those who profess to be His servants. When He calls your name, what will you say? When He calls your name, will you look to another for directions on how to respond and fulfill God's call? No one can explain and validate God's calling on you but Him. When He called you, He knew all about your abilities and inabilities. "*I know the plans I have for you says the Lord, plans for your welfare and not for harm, to give you a future with hope*" (Jer. 29:11). Maybe you are called to be a teacher, preacher, administrator, exhorter, giver, leader, encourager, or homemaker. Whatever your calling is, it is from God, not people. Know that you are able to fulfill this calling in spite of what you feel or think about yourself. You can do these things only through faith in Christ who gives you the necessary strength and ability. "*I am confident of this, that the One who began a good work in you will bring it to completion by the day of Jesus Christ*" (Phil. 1:6). Stop finding excuses to ignore God's call to stretch out, enlarge, and expand your abilities that you may serve the Lord. He has given you the power of His Spirit to accomplish His plan for your life. You have been empowered to hear His voice and obey His orders. Don't continue to ignore His voice when He calls you in the midnight hour by searching for a call you feel adequate enough for. If you lean on your own understanding, you will miss God's plan for your life.

DECEPTIVE FAVOR

"Don't let anyone deceive you in any way." II
Thess. 1:3

*"What is highly valued among men is detestable in
God's sight."* Luke 16:15

"I do not accept praise from men." John 5:41

*"How can you believe if you accept praise from one
another, yet make not effort to obtain the praise that
comes from the only God"* John 5:44

*"Jesus would not entrust Himself to them, for He
knew all men. He did not need man's testimony
about man for He knew what was in a man."* John
2:23-25

Beware of the praises and flatteries that you receive from
people, for they can influence you to believe what you
hear and cause you to miss out on what God is saying. If you
depend and rely on the favor of people to promote you or bring
you the opportunity you seek, you may be deceiving yourself.
Our promotions or advancements are not based on the favor
of men and women, but on the favor of God. It is the Lord
who raises us up and put us in a spacious place in life. It is not
by our might or power, not the favor of man that elevates us,
but it is the Spirit of the Lord that covers us with God's favor

(I Chron. 23:11-12). You need to know whether you are really believing God for a breakthrough or believing in the favor of those who speak well of your abilities. The Bible warns us to beware when people speak well of us, for the praises of man have caused many to presume that God will move on their behalf. Remember what the Apostle Paul said, *"No more boasting about men!"* (I Cor. 3:21). It is time to stop boasting about the favor you have from those in significant positions and how their influence can help you land the position you seek. If the favor you have with people of influence is from the Lord, you will receive the promotion, because He gives us favor with Him and man, but never intended for us to rely totally on the favor of man. This is a hard lesson to learn and can cause grief when what was expected doesn't materialize. My husband and I experienced this firsthand when He received an unusual amount of support and favor from several college and university presidents in his pursuit of a presidency. Great letters of recommendation were crafted, and numerous nominations were submitted to the search committee on our behalf, only to learn the limitations of the favor of men and women and how they can deceive you into believing their favor matters. As we recovered from the grief, we came to our senses and recognized how deceptive the praises and favor of people of influence can be. The only favor that matters is God's. There are no limitations to God's favor if it is His will to advance us in the capacity we desire. Our trust and faith must be in God alone. Promotions do not come from the favor and praises of men or women, promotions come from the Lord. Although ours was a painful experience, we are thankful to the Lord for its lesson and discipline. So, beware of the favor and praises you receive from those you highly esteem, for their influence is limited, but God's is unlimited. Don't be deceived into believing that your success is totally controlled by people of influence and power. No! If you know God and trust Him with all of your life, His plan will be to prosper you and not to harm you, but to give you hope and a future (Jer. 29:11). ♥

RECAPTURE YOUR DREAMS AGAIN!

"Do you believe I am able to do this? According to your faith will it be done to you." Matthew 9:28-29

Have you lost sight of what you believed God called you to become and do? What has distracted you from your dreams? Have you been deceived into believing that it is too late, or you are too old? Have you taken a detour that has taken you off the paths that lead to the fulfillment of your dreams? Who or what has robbed you of your dream to become a writer, motivational speaker, leader, artist, business owner, trainer, or preacher for God? Perhaps an enemy has broken in and robbed you of your dreams with deceptive distractions that detoured to another path, one that set you back instead of forward. Whatever the reasons, it is not too late to recapture what has been stolen. You don't have to let another setback keep you any longer, but you can push through and move forward. You can make a comeback with the measure of faith the Lord has given you. You may have experienced blind spots during your first attempts at pursuing your dreams, but know that the Lord is able to remove blind spots and give you renewed sight. Seek and you will find your dreams again; they were only hidden under all the lies and deceptive tactics of the enemy to distract you forever from believing they will come true. The following process was created to help you recapture your dream. All you have to do is reactivate your faith in God, who interprets and makes dreams come true. Take the evaluation test to refocus on truths from God's Word about the power of the words that come out of your mouth. Know that what you say can create what you receive in your life. *"Death and life are in the power of the tongue and those who love it will eat its fruit"* (Proverbs 18:21). You feast on words that give either life or death to your dreams. Pay attention to what you are speaking into your life and evaluate whether it agrees with God's promises. Know the power of the spoken word because it produces what it represents, whether good or bad. Our words fit in one of two categories: faith or fear. Listen closely to what you say and see if faith or fear is behind it.

ABOVE ONLY!

*"The Lord will make you the head and not the tail;
you shall be above only and not be beneath if you
heed the commandments of the Lord your God which
I command you today."* Deut. 28:13

A re you heavy laden under the loads of life? Why have you
chosen to let these loads weigh you down rather than give
them over to the Lord? You were created to live above the loads
of life, not beneath them. If you would just listen and obey what
the Lord says to you today, you will see blessings from above
overtaking you and freeing you from carrying that which brings
you down. Even the loads of despair and discouragement can
be given to the Lord and, in return, He will give you a peace
that passes all understanding to keep your heart and mind from
becoming downcast and depressed. Listen to what Jesus says
to all who let physical and emotional loads burden them down:
*"Come to Me, all you who labor and are heavy laden, and I will give
you rest. Take My yoke upon you and learn from Me, for I am gentle
and lowly in heart and you will find rest for your souls. For My yoke
is easy and My burden is light"* (Matt. 11:28-29). If you want to
get out from under loads that weigh you down, turn them over
to Jesus and He will pull you from underneath and place you
above, that you may be able to again set your eyes on things
above. Choose to listen to the Word of God and live on wings
of eagles waiting on the Lord to renew that which has been
weakened from loads of this life. If you ignore or disobey these
words of God, you are choosing to live beneath and not above

the burdens. *"The way of the unfaithful is hard. Every prudent* [wise] *man* [or woman] *acts with knowledge"* (Prov. 13:15). Be faithful to the Lord by embracing His way of life, the abundant life, in which you live above in your heart and mind before the Lord. We can have the mind of Christ, if only we put our minds on things above, the place we will spend eternity, and live free from the yokes and burdens that strip away the joy of the peace of God.

Dream Evaluation Form

The objective of this evaluation is to show you the types of words that uproot, rob, kill, or destroy your dreams. Be honest! Answering these ten questions could change your life. Take a minute to think on them and then ask Jesus for wisdom.

Is there a plan bubbling inside of you that you want to do?

Have you allowed the words of others to sabotage your dreams?

Are you speaking what you want to have?

What are you saying about your life?

Have your dreams withered and dried up from the roots?

What types of words are you storing up and treasuring in your heart?

Are you speaking blessings of God's promises or curses of doom?

Have you killed the "Goliath" in your life?

Have you cursed what God has blessed in your life?

Do you have a dream?

PRAISE POWER

"As they began to sing and praise, the Lord set ambushes against the men of Ammon and Moab." II Chron. 20:22

"About midnight Paul and Silas were praying and singing hymns to God" (Acts 16:25). *"Bless the Lord, you His angels who excel in strength, who do His word, heeding the voice of His word"* (Psalm 103:20).

If you want to see walls fall down that are blocking you from entering what God has promised you, if you want to see prison doors unlocked and chains falling off from those things that have held you captive, try praising God for being Almighty. Sing a new song to the Lord. Sing songs of about all the good the Lord has done for you. When you praise the Lord in the midst of the battle, and around the walls, or before the Red Seas of your life, He will give you a breakthrough and display His mighty power on your behalf. His ministering spirits move out when they hear our sacrificial praises and smell the fragrance of our songs Him. Take your position of praise and stand firm by continuing to praise Him no matter what you see that has mounted up against you. When we choose to worship the Lord instead of whining and complaining, miracles happen. It is through your praises that He is worshipped, not the praises you listen to that others are singing. Start singing your own praises to the Lord for all the great things He has done for your and for the great love that He has given you. Sing unto the Lord today and see Him set ambushes for your enemies, see Him crumble the walls before you, see Him unlock the prison doors and loosen your chains that you may be free to worship and praise Him. There is power in praise, but few of God's children have tapped into this power. Many have chosen to cry out in dismay and fear instead of praising Him for His faithfulness. He is seeking those who will praise Him in spite of the obstacles or opposition that stands in their way. Remain faithful to continue rejoicing in the Lord and you will see Him bring you through what troubles you. Remember this, *"God is our refuge and strength, A very present help in trouble"* (Psalm 46:1).

THE ACCUSER

"Josiah standing before the angel of the Lord and Satan standing at His right hand to accuse Him and the Lord said to Satan, 'The Lord rebuke you, O Satan! The Lord who has chosen Jerusalem rebuke you!' Now salvation, strength and the kingdom of our God and the power of His Christ have come for the accuser of our brethren, who accused them before our God day and night has been cast down. And they overcame Him by the blood of the Lamb and by the word of their testimony." Zech. 3:2; Rev. 12:10-11

"Who shall bring a charge against God's elect? It is God who justifies. Who is he who condemns? It is Christ who died, and furthermore is also risen, who is even at the right hand of God, who also makes intercession for us. Who shall separate us from the love of Christ?" (Romans 8:33-35a).

As Jesus said to the woman accused of adultery, He says us; *"… where are those accusers of yours?"* (John 8:10) Too many of God's children are suffering unnecessarily because they have believed the lie that God is not pleased with them because of sin and failings. If they stumble and fall into temptation and sin against God, but confess their sin and repent, the accuser continuously reminds them of their sin and floods them with feelings of shame, guilt, despair, self-condemnation, and depression, convincing them with a lie that God has not forgotten nor forgiven their sin. Feeling like a failure and disappointment to God and others pulls one farther down into a dark pit of self-imposed despair and affliction. Refusing to recognize the truth about God's amazing grace and forgiveness causes many to torture and imprison themselves. They refuse to rejoice over the truth that they are forgiven the moment they confessed their sins and asked God to forgive them. Many continue to punish themselves daily by ignoring the truth about God's amazing grace and merciful kindness. The truth will free you if you are one who has a hard time forgiving yourself for the mistakes you have made and sins you have committed. The truth is, *"If we confess our sins, He is faithful and just to forgive us our sins and to cleanse us from all unrighteousness"* (I John 1:9 KJV). Embrace forgiveness and free yourself from self-imposed afflictions. *"There is therefore now* [today] *no condemnation for those who are in Christ Jesus. For the law of the Spirit of life in Christ Jesus has set you free from the law of sin and of death"* (Rom. 8:1-2). The Lord says we are not condemned, but forgiven because of the cross of Christ. If Jesus doesn't condemn you, who will? Even the woman caught in adultery experienced the freeing power of Jesus' spoken word, *"Woman, where are those accusers of yours? Has no one condemned you? … Neither do I condemn you"* (John 8:10-11). So, ask yourself, who is condemning you and pointing fingers at your shortcomings? Who is saying, "You are a failure to God and others?" Who is saying, "You blew it!" Who is telling you that you can't please God? Who is saying, "You are losing your mind?" Who is saying, "You are defeated!" All these sayings are orchestrated from the father of lies, the devil, Satan, The Adversary, The Dragon, The Accuser, because there is no truth in him, just lies and illusions transmitted through the senses to make them appear real. But we are not bound to follow the dictates of our senses, because Christ freed us when He filled and sealed us with His Spirit. *"Now the Lord is the Spirit and where the Spirit of the Lord is, there is liberty"* (II Cor. 3:17). We were recreated by Christ when we received Him into our hearts; therefore, we walk by faith and not by sight (senses). Our feelings have been taken advantage of and used against us by the Accuser distract us from the truth that God is merciful and just, always abounding in mercy and grace. His grace forgave us, not because we did what pleased Him, but because He loves us. We lived alienated from God and gave Him our backs instead of our faces. We had no compelling desire to confess our sins and seek the cleansing power of His blood and word. God is merciful! He is not sitting up in heaven remembering all your sins, but He has blotted them out for His own sake and promised not to remember them. The Lord forgave the iniquity of His people and erased all their sin (Ps. 85:2). Go and walk in the forgiveness of God, confident that you have been forgiven by the only One who can forgive. Resist the Accuser by standing on the truth regardless of how bad you feel. Just know that feelings change like the weather and cannot be trusted as vehicles of truth. Jesus is the truth and if you would just focus your mind on Him during difficult times and emotional spirals, He will give you strength and power to rebuke the Accuser and resist his lies. Drawing near to God is standing on the truth when everything outside breathes lies. Live free from all forms of condemnation, especially self-imposed condemnation. Personally, I have given too much mental and emotional energy to listening and responding to this tormenting spirit of self-condemnation. I have wallowed in self-pity while listening to the Accuser remind me of my failings, but the truth told me to rise again after every fall. According to the Proverbs, a righteous man falls seven times but rises again. *"For Christ has set us free. Stand firm, therefore, and do not submit again to a yoke of slavery"* (Gal. 5:1). Walk in the truth that you are forgiven and no longer in bondage to condemnation.

LIVE LIMITLESS

"Go around and ask all your neighbors for empty jars. Don't ask for just a few." II Kings 4:3

"For this is what the Lord, the God of Israel says: The jar of flour will not be used up and the jug of oil will not run dry until the day the Lord gives rain on the land." (I Kings 17:14)

Stop allowing what you see to determine what you receive. Fix your eyes not on what is seen, the lack of resources, but on My unseen presence. For your needs are only temporary, but His presence provides lasting provisions. Remember what He said through Paul, *"Do not lose heart, though outwardly we are wasting away, yet inwardly we are being renewed day by day. For our light and momentary troubles are achieving for us an eternal glory that far outweighs them all"* (II Cor. 4:16-18). So, fix your eyes not on, the little that you think you have, but the abundance that He has given you. Think with no limits and begin to live a limitless life. The little oil and flour you have to survive on He will increase as you give it away to those in need. Giving away what you need is the way to limitless living, not holding onto or hoarding what you have. Resist the doom and gloom attitude that kept the children of Israel from receiving His promise to bring them into a land filled with all the provisions they could ever need, a land flowing with milk and honey. That same attitude tempted the widow of Zarephath who looked at what she had in her possession, a handful of flour and a little jar of oil when she had the opportunity to give away what she needed to someone in need. *"Then the word of the Lord came to him, saying, 'Arise, go to Zarephath, which belongs to Sidon, and dwell there. See, I have commanded a widow there to provide for you.' So he arose and went to Zarephath. And when he came to the gate of the city, indeed a widow was gathering sticks. And he called her and said, 'Please bring me a little water in a cup, that I may drink.' And as she was going to get it, he called to her and said, 'Please bring me a morsel of bread in your hand.' So she said, 'As the Lord your God lives, I do not have bread, only a handful of flour in a bin, and a little oil in a jar; and see I am gathering a couple of sticks that I may go in and prepare it for myself and my son, that we may eat it and die.' And Elijah said to her, 'Do not fear; go and do as you have said, but make me a small cake from it first, and bring it to me; and afterward make some for yourself and your son. For thus says the Lord God of Israel: The bin of flour shall not run dry, until the day the Lord sends rain on the earth.' So she went and did according to the word of Elijah; and she and he and her household at form many days. The bin of flour was not used up, nor did the jar of oil run dry, according to the word of the Lord which He spoke by Elijah"* (I Kings 17:8-16). We must think that nothing is too hard for the Lord to do when we add faith to His word. Our needs are an easy thing for the Lord to supply. As the widow of Zarephath obeyed what she was instructed to do for someone in greater need and received a miraculous increase of what she had on hand, so will we if we apply God's word in times of trouble. Limitless living requires faith. *"But without faith it is impossible to please Him, for he who comes to God must believe that He is, and that He is a rewarder of those who diligently seek Him"* (Heb. 11:6). *"Let us hold fast the confession of our hope without wavering, for He who promised is faithful"* (Heb. 10:23).

SWALLOW UP FEAR WITH FAITH

"Only do not rebel against the Lord. And do not be afraid of the people of the land because we will swallow them up. Their protection is gone, but the Lord is with us. Do not be afraid of them." Num. 14:9

To paraphrase Numbers 13, I believe this is what the Lord God was saying to the children of Israel through his servant Moses and to those of us who are called to a mission field:

When I tell you to go in to possess that which I promised, you must not look to the right or to the left to determine whether to go. And when you go to search and seek that which you believe I will do, and obstacles seem as large as giants or as wide as the Red Sea, remember Me. I will do according to your faith in Me. If you believe I can do the impossible, you will receive the impossible. Nothing is too hard for Me when you trust in Me with all your heart, soul, mind, and strength. I am the Almighty. I do mighty things on behalf of those who see Me with them. I am the only One who can take you into the land of the giants and cause you to swallow them up. It is your faith that will slay every giant that threatens you with fear. It is your faith that will part the Red seas in your life that you may be able to walk on dry ground into the land of promises that I have given you. Be strong and courageous to go when I say to go, and I will give you the desires of your heart. Remember, it is I who empowers you to swallow up those things that cause you to fear receiving what I have given you. Go up at once and take possession of the land, for you are certainly able to possess it through My presence. (see Num. 13:30)

Hear what the Lord Jesus said we have been given; *"Behold, I give you the authority to trample on serpents and scorpions and over all the power of the enemy and nothing shall by any means hurt you"* (Luke 10:19). We have been given power over fear to swallow it up with the faith the Lord has given us. The Apostle Paul reminds us of the kind of spirit we received when he said; *"For God has not given us a spirit of fear, but of power and of love and of a sound mind"* (II Timothy 1:7). We have the power to swallow up fear. Failure to use this power will allow fear to swallow us up into its torrents. *"There is no fear in love, but perfect love casts out fear because fear involves torment. But he who fears has not been made perfect in love"* (I John 4:18). Go forth today with boldness like a lioness and swallow up fear with the power of God's Holy Spirit. You are well able to overcome fear.

NEVER FORGOTTEN

"I will not forget you, See, I have inscribed you on the palms of my hand; your walls are continually before me." Isaiah 49:15-16

How many times have you felt abandoned by God in the darkest valleys of your life when suffering seemed to be your portion every day? When you prayed, did it seem like your prayers just bounced back and hit you on the head? Did you feel convinced enough to believe that God has forgotten you, that He has forsaken you, and that He won't answer your prayers? These are all lies designed to destroy your faith and trust in Him. The truth is, the Lord comforts His people and has compassion on His suffering ones. He knows when you are suffering because He looks at you in the palms of His hands and remembers you. If He wanted to forget you and me during our tough times, why in the world would He inscribe our names on the palms of His hands? It is time to stand up for truth and free yourself from the father of lies. God has not forgotten nor abandoned you and never will. Many of God's people suffered abandonment as children and have erected steel walls to protect them from being hurt again. They vowed within their hearts not to trust another again, because their trust was violated at a such young ages. They grew up doubting others because those who should have spoken words of love left. God has been treated with the same distrust as the parents who abandoned their children because He did not show up when they cried out in prayer for help. God has promised never to leave you nor forsake you. His promise is not based on our feelings or current circumstances. So, come out of the darkness of lies and see the light of the truth. Stand up and shake off the chains from your heart and mind that proclaim a different Gospel—one filled with distrust and suspicion. The Good News is, you are not forgotten. God knows you; He knows your name because you are inscribed in the palms of His hands. You are His child. He wants you to love Him so much that He put a reminder on your head of His faithfulness when suffering comes upon you. This will stop the tormentors of your mind from walking all over you with feelings of fear, depression, discouragement, self-pity, and defeat. The Lord says to you and me, *"I have put my words in your mouth and hidden you in the shadow of my hand"* (Isaiah 51:16). Speak the Word to the tormentors when they say you are suffering alone and that no one cares, not even God. Speak the truth and you will declare the glory of the Lord in the face of adversity. Learn to stand up, shake yourself off, and put on the strength that comes from faith and trust in the Lord's presence in times of trouble. *"God is our refuge and strength, a very present help in trouble. Therefore, we will not fear"* (Psalm 46:1-2).

LITTLE THINGS BECOME BIG THINGS

"What is that in your hand?" Exodus 4:2

"What do you have in your house?" 2 Kings 4:2

"How many loaves do you have?" Mark 6:38; 8:5

Now is the time to listen to God's word and believe what He is saying to you. He watches over His word to perform it. The Lord is faithful to perform whatever He promised you: *"I, the Lord have spoken, and I will surely do these things"* (Num. 14:35). It is time for us to stop limiting the Lord's promises according to the lack we see in our lives. Trust the little that you have and place it into his hands and he will make sure you have no lack of the things you need to survive the day's needs. Place what you have at your disposal into His hands and see His power increase the little that you have. Remember the works of the Lord and the demonstration of His power on behalf of those who took Him at His word; they did what He told them even if it sounded ridiculous. He turned a debt-ridden widow's bit oil into enough to pay her creditors with enough left over to provide for her and her family. It was the Lord who turned five loaves of bread and two fish into enough food to feed five thousand, as well as turning seven loaves of bread and a few fish to feed four thousand. In each case, a plentiful amount was left over. If we listen intently and obey what His word says, we will experience the same kind of increase in our lives. *"And my God shall supply all you need according to His riches in glory by Christ*

Jesus" (Phil. 4:19). He will do just as the Apostle Paul said: *"Now to Him who is able to do exceedingly abundantly above all that we ask or think, according to the power that works in us"* (Eph. 3:20). The Lord is your source and He is looking to bring glory to God's name by increasing what you placed in His hands. Give Him your wants, cares, and worries and He will provide all that you need today and forever.

TRUST

"Who among you fears the Lord and obeys the word of His servant? Let Him who walks in the dark, who has no light, trust in the name of the Lord and rely on His God." Isaiah 50:10

Why do we say and act as if our ways are hidden from the eyes of the Lord, as if He does not hear our cries? Do we not know that nothing is hidden from Him? Nothing in all creation is hidden from His eyesight, for everything is uncovered and laid bare before His eyes. Listen attentively to what David said about the Lord, *"Behold, the eye of the Lord is on those who fear Him, on those whose hope is in His mercy"* (Psalm 33:18). *"A man's ways are in full view of the Lord and He examines all His paths:* (Prov. 5:21). Why are we not putting our hope in the Lord, our Provider? Those who put their hope in Him lack nothing; no good thing will He withhold from them because He rewards those who diligently seek Him. It is foolish to trust in the arms of flesh above Him, because for a piece of bread a man will do you wrong (Prov. 28:21). Hear the warning of the prophet Jeremiah, *"Cursed is the one who trusts in man, who depends on flesh for His strength and whose heart turns away from the Lord. But blessed is the man who trusts in the Lord, whose confidence is in Him"* (Jer. 17:5, 7). *"Trust in the Lord with all your heart"* (Prov. 3:5). So, rely on Him and trust totally in Him for whatever needs you have today. He is the supply center for strength, peace, joy, and life. Trust in Him at all times and let goodness and mercy follow you all the days of your life. Let the

Yvette M. Jones

Lord be your confidence and He will keep you from falling into the traps of the enemy. Declare over your life today the words of David, _"I will trust and not be afraid. The Lord, the Lord, is my strength, and my song and has become my salvation"_ (Psalm 12:2).

WHOM ARE YOU AGREEING WITH?

"Can two walk together, unless they agree to do so?"
Amos 3:3

Whose instructions will you follow today? Whose voice will you hold dear to obey? Whose agreement will you endorse with your spoken word? The answer to these questions will reveal whom you follow in your responsibilities and duties. It takes two to form any agreement, whether you agree or disagree with the Lord your God. Our reactions to the daily events often disclose who we agree with and seek during hard times. Either we will agree with God or the Adversary. Job's reactions to continuous hardship revealed this truth, as he declared he agreed with God, therefore, he refused to curse God when the going got tough. He followed what he believed was God's instruction on handling suffering when he agreed that the Lord has the power to give and take away. Even though he faced great suffering and his friends turned against him, Job did not waiver in his focus on God and continued to praise Him no matter what he lost or how intense the pain. He made up his mind not to follow the voices of others or natural tendencies and curse God by agreeing with others, not even His wife, but trusted in God's faithfulness. When Job's friends accused him of not being acquainted with God and that he was not receiving instruction from God's Word, nor did he store up God's Words in His heart, Job continued to proclaim God's righteous judgment, *"He knows the way that I take; when He has tested me, I shall come forth as gold. My foot held fast to His steps; I have kept His way and not turned aside. I have not departed from the commandment of His lips; I have treasured the words of His mouth more than my necessary food ... He performs what is appointed for me"* (Job 22:21-22; 23:10-12, 14). What miracles we would see if we remained steadfast and unmovable in agreeing with the words of our Lord when adversity visited our lives. What radiance would reflect from our lives if we stood firm upon our faith, enduring until God showed up. We, too, would come forth as gold tried in a furnace. Do not be deceived! We were called to suffer as Christ suffered. What matters most is whether you agree to suffer patiently and continue doing good no matter how long it takes to hear God's voice. Or, will you agree with the adversary, the devil, who said this about Jesus when He hung on the cross, *"He trusted in God; let him deliver Him now if He will have Him; for He said, 'I am the Son of God'"* (Matt. 27:43). Does it feel like God has forsaken you during your time of great need? Do you really believe God has abandoned you? David identified with Jesus' feelings of abandonment when he wrote, *"My God, My God, why have You forsaken Me? Why are You far from saving me, from the words of my groaning? O My God, I cry by day, but You do not answer, and by night, but I find no rest* (Psalm 22:1-2). But Job refused to listen to his wife who said, *"Do you still hold fast to your integrity? Curse God and die!"* (Job 2:9). Do you curse God for the injustices you have suffered? The truth says, *"In this you greatly rejoice though now for a little while, if need be, you have been grieved by various trials, that the genuineness of your faith, being much more precious than gold that perishes, though it is tested by fire, may be found to the praise, honor and glory at the revelation of Jesus Christ"* (I Peter 1:6-7). Receive the end of your faith in God's faithfulness by walking in agreement with God, knowing that He will not tempt you beyond what you can bear. So, pray that the words of your mouth and the meditations of your heart are acceptable in the Lord's sight as you proclaim His faithfulness. He is a just God whose grace is sufficient to handle every difficulty we experience. Why not feast at His table today and make His Word your necessary food, declaring that you will live by every word that proceeds out of the mouth of God. Align your mouth and heart with His Word and surely goodness and mercy will follow you all the days of your life because you have chosen to eat at the table of the Lord and not at Satan's. Resist agreeing with the Adversary by drawing nearer to the Lord and he will flee from you. Guard your heart and your mind and bring every thought captive to the obedience of Christ.

PERFECT PEACE

"You will keep Him in perfect peace whose mind is stayed on You, because He trusts in You." Isaiah 26:3

I believe the Lord is telling us to stop leaving open the door of our minds for the thief to come in and steal our peace. Resist the devil's suggestive thoughts by fixing your eyes on the Lord who is the Author and Finisher of your faith. Trusting in Him requires doing all you can to stand on His word and not giving into the devil's lies that suggest He has abandoned you. Think on what He said, *"I will never leave you nor forsake you"* (Heb. 13:5).

Why are we so fearful about today and tomorrow? Do we not believe that the Lord is with us to keep us with His peace? Our peace is often disturbed because we have not chosen correctly today to put your trust in the Lord and not what we see, feel, or think. Remember, the Lord said to trust in Him with all our heart and mind, but we have allowed our mind to wander away from the truth. Those who enjoy perfect peace are those who have chosen to cast down every imagination that exalts itself against the knowledge of God and bring every thought captive to the obedience of Christ. Read and mark it in your bible the words of the Apostle Paul; *"For the weapons of our warfare are not carnal but mighty in God for pulling down strongholds, casting down arguments and every high thing that exalts itself against the knowledge of God, bringing every thought into captivity to the obedience of Christ, and being ready to punish all disobedience when your obedience is fulfilled"* (II Cor. 10:4-6). Perfect peace is available and accessible for you to enjoy today if you would just put your total trust in Jesus Christ and stop leaning and listening to your understanding. Self-reliance will not produce the peace that passes all understanding. Stop fearing what-ifs and believe in the presence of the Lord that is with you to provide, protect, and prosper you. King David said, *"I have been young, and now am old; Yet I have not seen the righteous forsaken, nor his descendants begging bread"* (Psalm 37:25). *"He is their strength in the time of trouble. And the Lord shall help them and deliver them ... Because they trust in Him"* (Psalm 37:39-40). Embrace My peace today and enjoy perfect peace. Remember this, *"But now in Christ Jesus you who once were far off have been brought near by the blood of Christ. For He is our peace"* (Eph. 2:13-14).

A RIPPLE EFFECT

"Keep away from the things devoted for destruction, so as not to covet or take any of the devoted [accursed] things and make the camp of Israel an object for destruction, bringing trouble upon it."
Joshua 6:18

What things do you possess that God has appointed for destruction? Does what you own cause God's anger to come down on your family? Are you doing anything to bring trouble upon your family? Have your choices contaminated those around you and caused them to become an object of destruction because of your unfaithfulness to God? It is time to clean house, the house of your heart and inventory its contents to see if you are hiding anything that God wants destroyed? Sin contaminates! Achan's actions contaminated all those around Him and brought defeat and destruction to his family. The whole clan, even all the children of Israel, was infected by his decision to covet what God said to destroy. God is not wishy washy with His instructions. He knows what He wants done. How much stuff around us has God told us to destroy or put on the altar? Do you have immoral movies that are filled with coarse language and pornographic images? Do you covet clothing and jewelry that you cannot afford? Do you hide your purchases because you know the money should be used for things more important, such as survival in hard times? Is your library filled with romance novels promoting unfaithfulness, lust, self-centered lifestyles, and pride? What music do you

92

listen to? Is it filled with profanity, sexual immorality, violence, unfaithfulness, and idolatry? When was the last time you conducted an inventory of your possessions to see if you have anything that God said should be destroyed? It is time to literally clean house for the Lord and sanctify yourself and those around you. Sin is when we know what God has told us to do and we disobey for reasons of greed, pride, and covetousness. Sin will steal the victories and joy God appointed for you. It will disrupt the unity within your family and remove God's presence from your life. This is what the Lord said to Joshua when He prayed for answers of why the few men of Ai were able to chase away and defeat the three thousand He sent to take the land: *"I will be with you no more unless you destroy the devoted* [accused] *things from among you ... There are devoted* [accused] *things among you ... you will not be able to stand before your enemies until you take away the devoted* [accused] *things from among you"* (Joshua 7:12-13). The Apostle Paul said, *"Jesus Christ is the same yesterday, today and forever"* (Heb. 13:8); and Malachi 3:6 says; *"For I am the Lord, I do not change."* He desires that we keep our houses and hearts clean from demonic influences that would hinder us from receiving the victory we have in Him. Our houses, our hearts, are God's homes on earth, *"Do you not know that your body is the temple of the Holy Spirit who is in you whom you have from God and you are not your own?"* (I Cor. 6:19). You see, we cannot do whatever we want with our bodies, because they have been bought by the Lord for a price we cannot repay. As Jesus told the lawyer, He tells us now how to live for God, *"You shall love the Lord our God with all your heart, all your soul, all your mind"* (Matt. 22:37). What thing(s) has the Lord been telling you to rid from your mind and heart? One way to find out is to ask yourself a few hard questions: "What hinders me from making God my highest priority?" "What tempts me to be unfaithful?" "What am I hiding or covering up?" "What do I crave more than serving the Lord?" "What collectibles possess my heart, soul, mind, and strength?" If God asked you to stay away from the things that He said should be destroyed, do it. If you disobey God, you will bring troubles of defeat and failure into the lives of those around you. Your loved ones will suffer the consequences of your choices. If you want to stand against your enemies and see God fight your battles, obey His will for your life. Victory comes only through obeying the Lord, no matter what it means giving up. It is time to clean house for the Lord and declare your devotion to Him. Remember what Jesus said, *"No one can serve two masters … You cannot serve both God and mammon"* (Matt. 6:24).

THE MEDICINE OF LAUGHTER

"A merry heart does good like medicine, but a broken spirit dries the bones." Proverbs 17:22

The power of laughter can rescue you from self-pity despair and show you the foolishness of your thoughts. This happened to me when the Lord used my husband to pull me out of the mood that had stolen my joyful attitude all day. He would cause me to laugh about what I was brooding over by saying things like, "Who is behind those feelings that are making you feel downcast? Who is making you feel like a failure?" I would burst out laughing when I saw the truth about joy and laughter being a source of strength. The truth that freed me was in Nehemiah 8:10-12: *"For this day is holy to our Lord. Do not sorrow, for the joy of the Lord is your strength. So the Levites quieted all the people, saying, 'Be still, for the day is holy; do not be grieved.' And all the people went their way to eat and drink, to send portions and rejoice greatly, because they understood the words that were declared to them."* The enemy of my soul got a foothold when I began to believe that no one cared for me or needed my counsel. He brought situations to mind of the times my daughters did not welcome my counsel on parenting and used that to suggest that they do not really care about me. When one daughter said she would call me back in a few minutes and didn't, I became prey for the enemy to discourage me with lies that pulled me down into the pit of despair and depression. But Paul said, *"Be sober, be vigilant; because your adversary the devil walks about like a roaring lion seeking whom He may devour"* (I Peter 5:7). He was after my joy that was ignited at the Damaris Carbaugh concert. Her songs brought me tears of joy as I thought on God's love and mercy. Her song, "He's Been Faithful!" broke down the wall that held back the tears. Then a phone call came from one of my daughters about counseling her sister on allowing so many people to hold her newborn. She felt her counsel hadn't been received or welcomed, and that she was less special to her sister than a stranger or her sister's in- laws. I could feel her pain and despair. Before I knew it, I began to think, "Where did I go wrong" in raising these two women. I thought I had demonstrated the importance of family, true family, not make-believe grandmothers, aunts, and uncles. One reaches out to improve the family ties and the other pulls away as if the family ties or closeness is a curse. Hearing the details of the conversation between my daughters quickly pulled my heart from joy to sorrow, from peace to self-condemnation, that led to momentary depression. By the time my husband arrived home from work, no sign of joy or peace was evident on my face. He thought I was suffering from a headache, but my heart was aching. A broken spirit dries the bones when the marrow of joy has flowed out. The Lord used my husband to make me laugh to rescue me from sliding deeper into feelings of despair. He said something funny at dinner that brought laughter up from the depth of my soul. I learned that you cannot be sad and laugh at the same time. My dark cloud was drifting away. The devil is always looking for ways to trick us into forgetting that nothing can separate us from the love of God. There is no greater love than God's love.

By the end of the day, I was restored and strengthened by the laughter of my husband and the joy of the Lord. If I had really listened to a warning I had read earlier in the day about the pit of self-pity and its strong pull, I would not have gone near it, but thanks be to God for His merciful kindness that is great toward me. He used my husband to deliver and rescue me with laughter.

Laugh more to avoid the pit of self-defeating thinking that leads to only self-pity and depression. It is hard to pull yourself out once you have fallen in. You need a rescuer, someone to make you laugh again. Learn to laugh more and the joy of the Lord will become your strength. *"Do not sorrow, for the joy of the Lord is your strength"* (Neh. 8:10).

I Can't, But God Can!

"The things which are impossible with men are possible with God." Luke 18:27

Know that God has given you the faith to accomplish His mission for your life. Listen to these words with your heart: *"God has dealt to each one a measure of faith"* (Rom. 12:3). Don't be afraid to step out of your comfort zones and walk into impossibilities with the Lord on your side. Peter stepped out of the boat and walked on water because he asked Jesus to prove Himself: *"And Peter answered Him and said, 'Lord, if it is You, command me to come to You on the water.' So he said, 'Come.' And when Peter had come down out of the boat, he walked on the water to go to Jesus"* (Matt. 14:28-29). Faith was essential when Peter stepped out of the boat and walked on water. Faith is important for each of us to achieve what God created us for. Keep in mind that each of us will have different levels of faith for different challenges, just like we all have been endowed by God with different gifts. *"There are diversities of gifts but the same Spirit. These are differences of ministries, but the same Lord. But the manifestation of the Spirit is given to each one for the profit of all ... for to one is given the world of wisdom through the Spirit, to another the word of knowledge through the same Spirit, to another faith by the same Spirit"* (I Cor. 12:4-9). God's Spirit lives in you and wants to move through you, but He can move only when faith is present: *"Without faith it is impossible to please Him, for he who comes to God must believe that He is, and that He is a rewarder of those who diligently seek Him"* (Heb. 11:6). As Jesus asked the two blind men, He is asking you and me, *"Do you believe that I am able to do this"* (Matt. 9:28)? Do you believe the Lord for the impossible? *"For with God nothing will be impossible"* (Luke 1:37). He can restore the barren womb; open doors to your dream job; provide for your education; make you a published author; sell your house or car; heal, deliver, and restore; He can even give a weight-loss plan tailored just for you! Ask yourself these questions to make sure you have faith in God: *"Let not your heart be troubled; you believe in God, believe also in Me"* (John 14:1).

Whatever area you struggle in, the only way to bring His power on the scene is to believe He can do the impossible. Apart from believing and trusting in Him, you cannot produce anything fruitful and successful in your life. Jesus said, *"Abide in Me ... as the branch cannot bear fruit of itself unless it abides in the vine, neither can you, unless you abide in Me"* (John 15:4). Abiding in Him means trusting and believing that He can do the impossible. And if you say, *"'Yes, Lord, I believe,' He will say, 'According to your faith let it be to you'"* (Matt. 9:29). The more we believe and the more we trust, the more we see Him and His ability to do the impossible.

I am confronted with a faith challenge whenever I read God's question to Jeremiah, *"Behold, I am the Lord, the God of all flesh. Is there anything too hard for Me"* (Jer. 32:27)? The appropriate response should be, *"Ah, Lord God! Behold, You have made the heavens and the earth by Your great power and outstretched arm. There is nothing too* [difficult] *for You"* (Jer. 32:17). Go in faith and believe that God can do through you what you can't do alone. He can move spiritual mountains out of your way. He can part the waters for you. He can prepare a table for you in the presence of your enemies. It is time to live out your faith fully and fly like an eagle. *"But those who wait on the Lord shall renew their strength; they shall run and not be weary, they shall walk and not lose faith"* (Isa. 40:31).

It Is Not Your Power That Succeeds

"Not by might, nor by power, but by My Spirit, says the Lord." Zech. 4:6

Think not that the work God has called and appointed you and me to complete can be done through our strength. We do not have the strength within ourselves to overcome the weaknesses of our flesh, especially during the times we are under spiritual attack. Jesus knew the weakness of our flesh when He told Peter how many times He would deny Him. Peter thought that desire and determination could make him faithful to the Lord until his death. Hear Peter's words; *"Even if all are made to stumble because of You, I will never be made to stumble … Even if I have to die with You, I will not deny You"* (Mark 14:29, 31)! Peter did not truly understand the words of Jesus when He said, *"The spirit is willing, but the flesh is weak"* (Matt. 26:41). Jesus gave this lesson when He asked His disciples to pray with Him for one hour. They did not understand the power of the flesh and how hard it could be to fight off sleep. We have faced the same temptation and been overtaken by sleep when a speaker or preacher has been long-winded, stretching the message to make a point. Years ago, churches use to conduct all-night prayer services and many fought off sleep and won, and some just gave in and fell asleep. When confronted, they would say they were just resting their eyes. Riiiight! The truth is they went to sleep on the Lord. But that is not my point; the truth is, when we become too weak to fulfill what we have openly declared in a great confession of our commitment to the Lord, we must understand that our own strength is unable to accomplish anything. Without His Spirit empowering and equipping us, the work we feel called to do will not be completed. It is not by human strength that we serve the Lord, but by His treasure, the extraordinary power of the Holy Spirit. It enables us to overcome being hard-pressed, perplexed, persecuted, struck down, or tempted to deny the Lord. If God's grace saved us without our merit or any personal contribution, it is by God's power that we can fulfill His calling on our lives. We are not above or better than Jesus, who acknowledged continuously that of Himself, He could do nothing without the Father. He acknowledged that the Father performed His purpose through Him and He only did whatever the Father did. Since we have the power of the Holy Spirit dwelling in us, why not acknowledge that we can of ourselves do nothing without the Holy Spirit. He enables and empowers us to accomplish what the Lord has for us today. So, when you become weak in the flesh, when you fall to sleep or stop building your life for the Lord, do not be discouraged. You are learning a valuable lesson: when you become weak in your abilities and strength, you are in a good place for the Lord to get the glory. Paul learned this lesson after repeatedly seeking the Lord for deliverance from the attacks he suffered. The Lord's answer to Paul, and us, is, *"My grace is sufficient for you, for My strength is made perfect in weakness"* (II Cor. 12:9). Learn to take pleasure in the fact that you can do nothing without the power of the Holy Spirit working through you. Your best strength is no match for the strength the Lord gives. In fact, He rarely uses anyone who depends on themselves to accomplish God's work; He chooses the weak. Paul learned this truth and changed from pleading to praising and from begging from the Lord to blessing Him. Paul said, *"Therefore most gladly I will rather boast in my weaknesses that the power of Christ may rest upon me. Therefore, I take pleasure in infirmities* [weaknesses, in reproaches, in needs, in persecutions, in distress], *for Christ's sake. For when I am weak, then I am strong"* (II Cor. 12:9-10). Wow! Our strength is made perfect in weakness. Weakness is strength when the excellence of the extraordinary power of the Holy Spirit is at work in us. So, stop trusting in yourself to accomplish what you believe the Lord has assigned and let the Spirit work by moving out of His way. Be confident of this very thing, that He who began a good work in you will complete it without reliance on your strength. He has enough strength and power to make you what He wants you to be, whether it is a writer, preacher, speaker, leader, artist, musician, business owner, parent, or prayer warrior. Always remember, *"Not by might, nor by power, but by My Spirit says the Lord of Hosts"* (Zech. 4:6), that you will accomplish the plans that the Lord has for you. *"For I know the thoughts that I think toward you, says the Lord, thoughts of peace and not evil, to give you a future and a hope"* (Jer. 29:11). *"Not that we are sufficient of ourselves to think of anything as being from ourselves, but our sufficiency is from God who made us sufficient as ministers …"* (II Cor. 3:5). God has equipped you to do the work before you today; let that glorious fact encourage and comfort you.

THE GLORY

"Whatever you do, do all to the glory of God." I
Cor. 10:31

When was the last time you spent the day thinking, speaking, and doing the things that glorify the Lord? Have you ever performed a self-study of your daily activities to see whether they glorify God or yourself? When suffering unexpectedly, do you endure, or do you give up? Who is getting the glory from your life? As the Holy Spirit presented this issue to me, I was challenged to do some soul searching. I am passing the challenge onto you. The scriptures are clear on who should receive the glory from our lives. It is also clear on who should not receive the glory. As I have searched the scriptures I have repeatedly read, *"He who glories, let Him glory in the Lord"* (I Cor. 1:31; 2 Cor. 10:17). Whether you realize it or not, we are all glory seekers longing to be lifted up and exalted by those around us. We are guilty of stealing God's glory when we grumble in our hearts when we are mistreated by those we have served. How many times have you worn Martha's shoes and said, *"Lord don't you care that my sister, brother, husband, wife, children or friend has left me to serve alone. Look, all they do is sit around waiting for me to wait on them without showing any sensitivity to my need to be served sometime. Lord, why don't you tell them to help me?"* I have worn Martha's shoes more than I care to admit and have complained in my heart to the Lord when I felt overwhelmed by the demands of others. I have entertained thoughts that fed my sense of feeling unappreciated, unloved, and taken for granted. I have even dropped hints in the hopes that they would come to their senses and see that I have needs too. But I never realized how self-centered my attitude was and how this kind of thinking put me on a quest to seek glory and exaltation from man. I did not think I was depriving God of His due, but when I chose not to rejoice in the midst of times of suffering while serving, I was withholding from God His glory and the opportunity to care for me. The times I felt my good deeds were taken for granted or unappreciated, I wanted to go on strike and do nothing or give nothing to those who didn't pat me on the back. I felt tired of the scales being weighted down on my side with good deeds and few deeds on the side of the receiver of my good. The Word of God revealed the truth and made clear to me God's will for my life today. We are all called to do good for others as if we are doing it unto the Lord and to resist feeling discouraged, depressed, or upset when our deeds go unnoticed or unrewarded. The Lord will reward all the good we have done with the right heart and attitude, when He is the One to get the glory. God did not call us to seek our own glory, but as Paul said, we should speak not to please men but God, nor should we seek glory from men or others (I Thess. 2:4-6). The calling to live every day to give God the glory is the gospel truth that Paul confirmed when He said, *"For do I now persuade me or God? Or do I seek to please men? For if I still pleased men, I would not be a bondservant of Christ"* (Gal. 1:10). Know that those who lift themselves or another up as deserving the glory will not receive the glory, because it is only God's to give (II Cor. 10:18). Resist the temptation to please others for your own profit or glory, but give all glory to God in all you do and say today. Remember what Jesus said, *"How can you believe, who receive honor from one another, and do not seek the honor* [glory] *that comes from the only God? He who speaks from himself, seeks his own glory; but he who seeks the glory of the One who sent Him is true; I do not receive honor* [glory] *from men"* (John 5:44-45; 7:18). Pray this: "Lord, glorify yourself through my life today that God may get the glory. Deliver me from my evil desires and deeds that focus on self-profiting from the good I do for others and deliver me from motives centered on honoring and glorifying myself, that I may truly give your name all the glory and all the honor. Help me to free my family and friends from all my secret motivations to reward myself for the good that I have done in serving them. Lord, I am weak in this area and desperately need you to keep me from stealing your glory. Thank you, Jesus for your mercy and grace toward me when I fail to give the glory to God. Amen."

Soul Food

"Your word was found, and I ate them, and Your word was to me the joy and rejoicing of my heart."
Jeremiah 15:16

Do you feel empty inside, but don't know why? Have you tried the things suggested by others or the media to find fulfillment and satisfaction, but come up dry? Has pursuing diet plans, exotic vacations, new clothes, expensive cars and jewelry, that dream home, higher degrees, a relationship or children, executive titles and positions, publishing a book, public speaking opportunities, wigs and weaves, acrylic nails, or expensive spa treatments all seemed to leave a void after the thrill of the pursuit has worn off? Have you felt like singing the old song, "I can't get no satisfaction?" Do you seemingly have everything the world says is enough to make you happy and fulfilled, yet find yourself still feeling empty? This has been my experience over the years as I enjoyed the momentary pleasures of each blessing. I have enjoyed many of the things the world promises will bring a happy and contented life, but often found myself battling a spirit of discontentment. It was not that I needed more adventures or stuff; what I was missing was soul food. Not the ethnic food that represents the African American culture, but the food that feeds the spiritual soul. So, I quit my executive job with all the travel perks and set myself in front of the Word of God. I prayed and cried to have my soul repaired from the exhaustion of seeking worldly fulfillment and restored and refilled with God's Word.

Refocus your eyes on the Light and fill your ears with things that bring life. Live as a child of Light. Listen to the words of Jesus, *"You are the light of the world … let your light so shine before men that they may see your good works and glorify your Father in heaven"* (Matt. 5:14-16). Beware of what you allow your eyes to see and ears to hear. Fix your eyes on Jesus and hear what His Spirit says to you today and the darkness that has surrounded you will loosen its grip and flee. *"Blessed are your eyes for they see and your ears for they hear; for assuredly I say to you that many prophets and righteous men desired to see what you see and did not see it and to hear what you hear and did not hear it. He who has ears to hear, let Him hear what the Spirit says"* (Matt. 13:16-17; Rev. 2:17). *"Finally, brothers, whatever is true, whatever is honorable, whatever is just, whatever is pure, whatever is lovely, whatever is commendable, if there is any excellence, if there is anything worthy of praise, think about these things"* (Phil. 4:8).

BE CAREFUL WHAT YOU SEE AND HEAR!

"The eye is the lamp of the body. If your eyes are good your whole body will be full of light. But if your eyes are bad, your whole body will be full of darkness. If then the light within you is darkness, how great is that darkness!" Matt. 6:22-23

You have probably heard the children's song, "Be careful little eyes what you see. Be careful little ears what you hear." I believe those words are for all God's children today, regardless of age. It is important to protect carefully our eyes and ears from the pollutants of this world. Watching images on T.V. or movie screens that are covered in darkness and listening to the fear and death-filled words can fill our mind's eyes and mouths with that which corrupts and destroys the light of Christ in us. It would be like hiding our light under a bushel, and that bushel is the dark things of this world that Satan uses to shift the light of good out of the people of God to get them comfortable with darkness. The enemy of our soul wants us to love darkness rather than light because light exposes darkness and reveals the truth. If you read and listen to everything the critics say about you, you will soon become fearful and self-critical because you will begin to take on the very nature of those you have given your ear and eyes to. In Ecclesiastes 7:21, we are warned to avoid listening to every word people say because you will hear them curse you. If a pro athlete listens to disgruntled fans because He makes a mistake that cost his team a game, that athlete would live in constant torment and fear. If you watch and listen to the news about all the killings and violence in the world, you will become filled with fear and question your safety and security. Watch a movie about a plane crash before you are to fly somewhere and see how the power of suggestion will influence your thoughts during your flight. This why it is so important to guard your eyes and ears, because they are the gateways to your heart, soul, and mind. Jesus said, *"Consider carefully what you hear for with the measure you use, it will be measured to you-and even more"* (Mark 4:24 NIV). I like the NKJV: *"Take heed what you hear. With the same measure you use, it will be measured to you and to you who hear more will be given."* Although this verse is talking about hearing the Word of God, the warning can be applied to listening to negative, fear-filled, and destructive words. Too often, we have allowed our eyes and ears to become dumping grounds for the trash of this world. No wonder we question the will of the Lord when overwhelming darkness floods our minds and hearts. For too long we have allowed our eyes to view the world's sex, violence, greed, and spiritual wickedness and call it entertainment. We have failed to realize that our very lives are being influenced by all this darkness. Ever wonder why you sometimes feel down and negative. Could it be connected to what you have watched on TV or listened to on the radio or from the mouths of those who promote the doom and glooms of our society? I have had to change the channel on some Christian radio programs that talk a lot about suffering and sorrows and put on praise music in order to shift my mind to God's goodness. I know these broadcasts are trying to reach out to the hurting and encourage them to put their hope in God, but on the days in which I'm battling to ignore fearful thoughts, I have to take back the control over what I listen to at that moment of vulnerability. My beloved sisters and brothers, it is time for you to take back controls from the world and change the channel to that which uplifts and encourages you and pleases God. Stop feasting on all the violent and sex-laden things that promise false pleasure or fulfillment. The missing link is not anything the world has to offer, but the Bible, the Book of Life, the Soul Food book. All I have to do is open it and eat what God says was not written to me, but for me. Reading the many references to God's fulfillment for me brought tears to my eyes because I saw the foolishness of spending so much time and energy seeking the wrong things to fill my innermost being.

Job knew God's Word was soul food when He spoke these words to His accusers/friends: *"I have treasured the words of His mouth more than my necessary food"* (Job 23:12). Have you treasured God's Word more than the food of diets, the food of the American Dream, the food of education, the food of wealth, the food of health and fitness, or the food of world travel? What is feeding your appetite each day? Whatever you consume is what feeds you. If you spend much of your time watching T.V., you are likely getting your daily bread from the world. It has been said by many that we are what we read, we are what we eat, we are what we listen to, and we are what we think. For example, eating a daily diet of talk shows filled with gossip, injustice, unfaithfulness, and medical crises will set your mind on those things and away from God's truths. When we watch the news and hear of the crime that fills our city streets and the senseless killings around the world, we can begin to feel fearful and insecure. God's plan was never for us to survive off any other soul food that what comes out of His Word. He created the right kind of food to nourish the soul of every human being. Jesus Christ proclaimed this when He was tempted in the wilderness by the devil, *"It is written, man shall not live by bread alone, but by every word that proceeds from the mouth of God"* (Matt. 4:4). Eat the right kind of soul food for today and enjoy the presence of the Lord, a presence that gives peace and contentment in the midst of a troubled world. Be like a deer and pant for God's Word to quench your thirsty soul. Drink the water of His Word and never thirst again. Let your innermost being be filled and saturated with His Word. Start with small portions, such as reading a chapter of Proverbs and Psalms a day and your appetite will increase to wanting more, because His Word is fast acting and more powerful than anything the world can offer. I grew up eating my culture's soul food of fried chicken, potato salad, collard greens, crackling cornbread, chitterlings, pigs' feet, okra, and candied yams, all of which were loaded with calories and fat, but truly satisfied the taste buds. It was my normal diet and I knew of nothing better. It was not the healthiest diet though, and many have adhered to it in the name of cultural norms and succumbed to diabetes, high blood pressure, and cancer. After losing many loved ones to premature death, I have changed to mostly healthier foods, but strive to eat what is good for the soul first. If you neglect feeding your soul the right kind of soul food needed to conquer the struggles of the day, you will go to bed feeling empty within because you chose the wrong diet. Declare what Jesus said: *"I will not live by bread alone, but by every word that comes from the mouth of God, my Father."* His Word is my necessary food.

WHO IS FEEDING YOU?

"Open your mouth and eat what I give you."
Ezekiel 2:8

This key verse was spoken to Ezekiel, the Prophet, before the Lord stretched out His hand to give him a scroll. The Lord was commissioning Him to speak to a rebellious people. Before he left, God spoke to Him by breathing on Him, and the Spirit of God empowered Him to carry out his task. The amazing thing about the story of Ezekiel's assignment is that he ate from the hand of God. The Lord God fed him by putting into his mouth what he needed to speak out of his mouth. The Lord said to Him, *"'Son of man,' He said to me, "eat what is before you, eat this scroll; then go and speak ..." (Ezek. 3:1).* Ezekiel had to do something to receive what God was giving him, so he opened his mouth to eat the scroll of God's Word. The words he ate fed his innermost being and filled his stomach as the Lord said it would. It became sweet as honey to his mouth. If you have a sweet tooth, why not let God fulfill your craving for sweets? David had the same experience when he ate God's Word and proclaimed it was, *"Sweeter than honey and the honeycomb. Moreover, by them, your servant is warned and in keeping of them there is great reward"* (Psalm 19:10-11). When Jeremiah found God's Word, He ate it and found it to be the source of joy and gladness. Job ate God's Word and found it to be more fulfilling than the food that feeds the physical body. In Revelation, John took and ate a little book from the hand of an angel and found it to be as sweet as honey in his mouth, but bitter in his stomach. All of God's messengers were called and commissioned to eat in order to speak for the Lord. They literally became what they ate because the fruit of their mouths revealed what was stored within them. They were known by their fruit, the words of their mouths. Why not open your mouth and let God feed you His Word? He has a word that He wants you to proclaim to those He sends you to. Many need a word from the Lord and if someone is not sent, how will they hear the Good News of God's mercy, grace, and love? The food God feeds you will give you and others life. Jesus said, *"The words that I speak to you are spirit and they are life"* (John 6:63). If Jesus lives in you, His Spirit is also in you, so the words you speak can bring life or death to those you speak to, but the power depends on whose words you have consumed. Feedings from the hand of the world are filled with death because they destroy life, but feedings from the hand of God give life, which, when shared, produce more life. Death and life are in the power of the tongue and people eat the food they crave. Open your mouth wide to God and He will help you to crave Him alone. Solomon said, *"The righteous eats to the satisfying of his soul, But the stomach of the wicked will be in want"* (Prov. 13:25). If you want to eat well, let the Lord fill your mouth with His Word and the fruit of your mouth will satisfy your soul. Feasting on God's Word and spreading it through spoken words is the only way I know to satisfy our souls with the sweetness of honey and give us a sweet day—one covered with God's honeycomb.

WORK VERSUS WORSHIP

*"There remains a Sabbath-rest for the people of God;
for anyone who enters God's rest also rests from His
own work just as God did from His."* Hebrews 4:9

*"There is a time for everything, a season for every
activity under heaven."* Eccl. 3:1

I believe one of the greatest hindrances to worshipping the
Lord is work. We may as well admit that we lack discipline
in this area and often find our lives out of balance. Our days
are filled with multiple activities that leave us with little time
for the kingdom of God. We are driven by mental slave drivers
and foremen every waking hour and become too busy to hear
the still, small voice of the Holy Spirit. When was the last
time you sat quietly, alone, listening for a fresh word from the
Lord? During your prayer times, do you wait silently for a few
minutes until the Lord speaks? What is the will of the Lord for
you today? Do you know He has a plan for you to fulfill today?
Reading the words of Isaiah the prophet, Paul the Apostle,
Solomon, and Moses, I could hear the Spirit, the Counselor,
saying it is time to wake up to the voice of the Lord. The Spirit
is crying out from the high places for the people of God to
"awake and clothe yourself in strength" (Isa. 51:9; 52:1). It is time
to wake up to the truth and be freed from the lies that have
put your mind and heart asleep to the presence of the Lord.
Looking in Exodus, chapters 5 and 6, the children of Israel had
physical slave drivers who pushed them to work 24/7 so they

would be too busy and too worn out to think on the Lord God. Whenever they took time for God and the enemy heard of it, the work was made harder in order to keep them from paying any attention to the call to sacrifice time to worship the Lord. Today, many of God's children believe that not being busy all the time makes they look lazy. This is a lie from the enemy to keep us for meditating on the Lord. The key to keeping work balanced with the Lord's will is to commit our work to the Lord and let Him establish our plans (Prov. 16:3). So, why not start tomorrow by worshipping the Lord and not running to work. Resist the temptation to give the Lord the leftovers of your day; give Him your best, the first fruits of your time. You will see His mighty outstretched arms move on your behalf. Then you will be able to enter into the rest that is prepared for those who live a balanced life of worship and work.

Boastings Have No Guarantee

"Do not boast about tomorrow for you do not know what a day may bring forth." Proverbs 27:1

How many times have you said, "Next year I (we) will do_"; "Next month I (we) are going to____"; or "Tomorrow I (we) will_____." When you spoke these or similar statements, did you felt confident that your plans would succeed? It is amazing how many conversations you hear in the workplace, marketplace, and church about what people are going to do for a particular holiday or vacation. Sometimes a competition arises unknowingly as people portray their holiday celebrations or vacations as more exotic or fantastic than others. Ever wonder what is behind this form of communication? Are we revealing how insecure we are about our identity and significance? Are we just proud of what we do and want to sound a trumpet to focus attention in our direction? I was serving at a church event to feed the poor and could not drown out the conversations around me. The elder couples were going back and forth sharing stories and plans for upcoming vacations at exotic locations. It sounded like they were in a contest for who had the most exciting retirement lifestyle. The types of vacations discussed revealed who had the most disposable income because of the mentioning of waterfront villas, sailboats, and exotic vacation spots. The man working on my team informed me that he was planning on taking his five grandchildren and their parents to Disneyland. Why he felt compelled to tell me this, I don't know. I was just there to pack as many seeds for the poor in

Africa as I could during my scheduled time. I am not pointing fingers, nor judging others, but just showing you the truth that I learned when I was guilty of indulging in the same practices. I believe the motive behind such boasting is the fear of being excluded and not accepted by those we highly esteem. Why do we feel our stories have to be bigger and better than those of others? Why do our vacations or holidays have to be the best one can enjoy? Why do we feel the need to brag? Nothing in our tomorrows is guaranteed. We are told not to boast about tomorrow because we do not know what a day will bring forth into our lives. Boasting about such things comes without a guarantee, and will not bring the results you desire—for people to look up to you. You will not receive praise, but criticism for being so insecure and self-centered. Most people do not want to hear about your travel plans or big purchases. James said, *"Come now, you who say, Today or tomorrow we will go to such and such a city, spend a year there, buy and sell, and make a profit; whereas you do not know what will happen tomorrow. For what is your life? It is a vapor that appears for a little time and then vanishes away. Instead, you ought to say, 'If the Lord wills, we shall live and do this or that. All such boasting is evil'"* (James 4:13-16). I believe that what makes boasting evil is that it looks down on the less fortunate and exalts oneself. This is evil in God's eyes. Jesus said, *"For what is highly esteemed among men is an abomination in the sight of God"* (Luke 16:15). God hates pride. Jesus said this many times, especially when He said that He came not to be served, but to serve and that to be great in God's kingdom is to be a servant of all. In order to have a servant's attitude, you have to become like a kernel of wheat and fall to the ground and die to self. It is time to lay aside all your boastful ways, to forsake such foolishness, and pursue righteousness by doing what is right in God's sight. He is not impressed with your stories of adventure, celebration, and success. He is impressed when you submit your whole being to Him by offering yourself up daily to Him as a living sacrifice. If you tend to boast or provide unsolicited information, pray these words; "Let the words of my mouth and the meditation of my heart be acceptable in Your sight, O Lord. Open my lips and my mouth shall show forth Your praise, not mine. Set a guard ... over my mouth; keep watch over the door of my lips. Do not incline my heart to any evil thing such as boasting, to practice wicked works ... and do not let me eat the delicacies [bragging rights] of those around me. For only through Your strength and the Power of Your Spirit will I overcome bragging about what I have no control over in my life today and tomorrow. In Your name, I make this petition and declare that only Your grace comes with a guarantee that is sufficient for all my weaknesses. Amen."

EXCLUDED, IGNORED, REJECTED

"Love your enemies, do good to those who hate you,
bless those who curse you, pray for those who mistreat
you … If you love those who love you, what credit is
that to you?" Luke 6:27, 32

How should we respond when we are mistreated, excluded from the conversation, ignored when we give input into a discussion, treated like a child, talked about in the negative, and given looks of hatred from those we work with? The above experiences happen to everyone at one time or another. I have found one way to cope with them in the Bible, and it sounds easy, but is difficult when feelings tempt you to do otherwise. Luke says to love others in spite of their unloving ways. He says the way to love is to bless them when you feel like cursing them, to give when you feel like ignoring, to pray when you feel like taking revenge, and to do good when you feel like doing bad. This is the opposite of the world's standards: an eye for an eye, overcome evil with evil, insult for insult, take revenge into your hands. Following the world's ways will have you spending your life fighting everyone who mistreats you and never seeing the freedom of mercy and grace. Follow God's Word and love—and you will be blessed.

Self-Denial

"If anyone wants to become My follower, let them deny themselves and take up their cross daily and follow Me. For those who want to save their life will lose it, and those who lose their life for my sake will save it." Luke 9:23-24

There is a cost in following the Lord. You may have thought that following Him would make your life run smoothly and be free of pain or suffering, adversities or afflictions. You have sought the Lord in your despair and desperation because someone told you He would give you a life of abundance, a good and prosperous life. When you lacked things, you were invited to come to Jesus and receive. If you were sick, you were told to seek Jesus for healing. These invitations were given in love, but too often, the point of them was to simply seek deliverance from suffering. For many, being a child of God has seemed to increase their trials and troubles. I have heard many say, "Don't pray for patience, it's like asking for trouble." Why do we want to follow Jesus without suffering? Is that the kind of example He left us? If He learned obedience through the things He suffered, and we are not better than Him, why should we not suffer? We must admit that we do not want to suffer for anyone, not even the Lord. If this is the way you have been thinking, you have been deceived, lied to, and far removed from the truth. According to the gospels, and Paul and Peter, we have been called to suffer in order that we may be coheirs with Christ. We are blessed if we suffer for Jesus' name, *"Blessed are you when they revile and persecute you and say all kinds of evil against you falsely for My sake. Rejoice and be exceedingly glad, for great is your reward in heaven"* (Matt. 5:11-12). A disciple is not above his teacher, nor are we above the Lord. If Jesus suffered, we will suffer. *"Beloved, do not think it strange concerning the fiery trial which is to try you, as though some strange thing happened to you; but rejoice to the extent that you partake of Christ's sufferings"* (I Peter 4:12-13). It is time to become a grain of wheat, fall to the ground, and die so as to become fruitful in living for the Lord. Our life is not our own to live as we choose. It has been paid for with the life of Christ. If we want Christ to be seen in our lives, we must die to the "it's all about me" syndrome. Christ did not die to promote the self-life, which is what set humanity on the course of destruction, but He died to save humanity from themselves. *Know that the Lord made us and not we ourselves* (Psalm 100:3). He died for all, that those who live should live no longer for themselves, but for Him who died for them (II Cor. 5:15). It is time to die daily to the things that draw us into ourselves and cause us to forget the love God has for us. He knows what's best for us. It is time to die to a self-centered life by offering up our hearts, minds, souls, and strength as living sacrifices to the Lord. Give Him your heart and let Him use you to transform lives through the fruit produced in you. People need to see the ambassadors of Christ carrying figs from heaven to feed their hungry souls and carrying living water to quench their thirsty souls. Be the one to say, *"Here I am, send me"* (Isaiah 6:8). Declare to the world that your selfish have been crucified with Christ, that He may live through you. When the going gets tough and self-centered thoughts close in on you, recite the words of the Apostle Paul, *"I have been crucified with Christ; it is no longer I who live, but Christ lives in me; and the life which I now live in the flesh I live by faith in the Son of God who loved me and gave Himself for me"*

(Gal. 2:20). We show our greatest love for the Lord when we do as He has done for us and lay down our lives for His will and His ways. Until we die to self, we will remain fruitless fig trees out of season, having nothing to nourish the hungry souls that come into contact with us.

EVER PRESENT!

"God is our refuge and strength, an ever-present help ..." Psalm 46:1

Why do we struggle to believe that God is with us during our tough times? Why do we believe our feelings more than the promises of God? As God's people, we are called to live by faith and not by emotion. Yet, we suffer much despair when we allow our feelings to make us doubt God's faithfulness. He watches over His word to perform it. He is not a man that He should lie. As the Lord said to the children of Israel, He says to you and me, *"Why do you say ... and complain, O Israel, my way is hidden from the Lord; my cause is disregarded by my God?"* (Isaiah 40:27). *"Nothing in all creation is hidden from God's sight; Everything is uncovered and laid bare before the eyes of Him to whom we must give account"* (Heb. 4:13). It is time to adopt the attitude of Father Abraham and give glory to God. Abraham was fully persuaded that God could do what He had promised (Rom. 4:21). If the Lord promised never to leave us or forsake us, we can bank on it and know that we are not alone in our sufferings. Hear the promise through the prophet Isaiah, *"Do not fear, for I am with you; do not be dismayed, for I am your God. I will strengthen you and help you; I will uphold you with my righteous right hand"* (Isa. 41:10). *"As I was with Moses, so I will be with you; I will never leave you nor forsake you. Be strong and courageous! Do not let this Book of the Law depart from your mouth; meditate on it day and night, so that you may be careful to do everything written in it. Then you will be prosperous and successful.*

Have I not commanded you? Be strong and courageous. Do not be terrified; do not be discouraged, for the Lord your God is with you wherever you go" (Joshua 1:5-9). Wow! This says it all; God has given us the same promise that He gave Joshua and the children of Israel, which proves what is written, that the Lord is the same yesterday, today, and forever. The Lord is with us *wherever* we go—at work, at school, or at home—God is ever-present. So, resist the temptation to doubt the promises of His presence and believe despite what your senses say and walk by faith and not by sight. The last promise the Lord Jesus Christ gave to the disciples was this: *"And surely, I am with you always, to the very end of the age"* (Matt. 28:20).

WHY WORRY?

"Who of you by worrying can add a single hour to His life?" Matthew 6:27

In each new day and season of my life, I am tempted to worry about many things. In order to start the day with a right attitude, it is essential that I seek the counsel of the Lord through reading the scriptures and praying. Those two things will renew my mind and feed my soul. If I didn't start my day with Jesus, I would be more inclined to worry over my concerns or see things through my own eyes.

Over the years, I have struggled with worrying about so many things, especially when it comes to meeting the needs of others or giving myself to hospitality. I cannot tell you all the times I have been led to read Matthew 6:25-34 and Luke 10:38-42 and listen to what the Lord says about the temptation to worry. On one of those days, I had to run to the Word of God first, because the preparations and To-Do list for a Christmas party felt like a Goliath that threatened to overwhelm me with failure and fear with every passing thought. In reading about Martha being anxious and worried about the preparations for her dinner party, I realized that the problem was not the preparations, nor was it the distractions or lack of help. It was my lack of faith in the only One who can strengthen me to do all things. When fear is at the root of my worries and anxieties, faith and peace are absent from my heart. The peace of God comes when I cast all my worries on the Lord and believe that He does care for me. So, I have chosen not to run to the tasks on my To-Do list, but to run to the scriptures for a word of counsel on handling all the tasks of today. Even though the Christmas party was just two days away, I could not worry about tomorrow. I had only that day to seek first the Kingdom of God and His righteousness by putting my faith in Him to strengthen me to do what was needed. When Jesus asked His disciples, *"Where is your faith?"* (Luke 8:25), I felt this question was for me too. Then I realized that the issue wasn't what I did to serve the Lord, but whether I did it in reverence and faith. It was clear to me that my anxiety and worry meant that I wasn't operating in faith, but in doubt and fear, which distracts and divides the mind, making it unstable in all its thinking. Praying for wisdom and guidance in handling the tasks of today is a must if we are to walk in the peace that passes all understanding. We need to pray daily for wisdom and believe that God will grant the desire of our hearts, which is to please Him, and the only way that can happen is to handle every task believing the Lord is with us. Faith is the only way to banish worry and keep it from stealing our peace. So, do as James 1:5-8 says: *"If anyone of you lacks wisdom, He should ask God, who gives generously to all without finding fault, and it will be given to Him. But when He asks, He must believe and not doubt, because He who doubts is like a wave of the sea, blown and tossed by the wind. That man should not think He will receive anything from the Lord; He is a double-minded man, unstable in all He does."* Wow! Worry makes you unstable in your thinking, but when you wait on the Lord and trust in Him to guide you; He will show you how to complete the tasks with peace and joy, no matter the circumstances. This has been my reward from the Lord when I have listened to His counsel and allowed Him to guide me in what task to do and what not to do. I found that it took less time to do what was needed and I enjoyed the doing without having an anxious heart. Truly, this is all about faith versus fear and you have to make a choice today whether you will walk by faith or run in fear. *"And without faith it is impossible to please God, because anyone who comes to Him must believe He exists and that He rewards those who earnestly seek Him"* (Heb. 11:6).

The Walk Of Love

"Be kind to one another, tenderhearted, forgiving one another, even as God in Christ forgave you ... Therefore be imitators of God as dear children and walk in love." Ephesians 4:32; 5:1

How do you walk in love when your heart is grieved by wrongs suffered while doing good? Is there any loophole that says it is ok not to forgive? When your children continue to disobey, should you forgive them? What about forgiving the unjust criticism of those who attack with words in an effort to destroy your joy. Should you forgive? Should you forgive abandonment and abusive behavior inflicted upon you during your childhood? Should you forgive your parent who never asked for your forgiveness before they died? Forgiving is one of the hardest things I have ever had to do. It is a process that takes years to learn and yet is never mastered it because it is much easier to hold a grudge and nurse negative emotions. One thing I learned about nursing a grudge rather than releasing someone's guilt: I become the one who suffers the most. The person who committed the offense has gone on with their life and is not thinking about how you feel. Refusing to forgive holds you in the grip of the torturers who remind you daily of how it felt to be offended. You are the one in bondage, not your offender. The offense that has passed will eat you alive by killing the love you are capable of giving. Love dies when we do not forgive. The example in the gospel of Matthew makes it clear why it is important to forgive. The wicked servant who begged his master to forgive his debt was freely granted his petition with compassion, but when his own servant asked for mercy, he refused. He quickly forgot how similar his plea was to the one pleading to him to be forgiven. He did not realize that the opportunity to forgive was a test that revealed the condition of his heart, whether he would do unto others as it had been done unto him. As Jesus said to the wicked servant, He says to us, *"Should you not have had compassion on your fellow servant just as I had pity on you?"* (Matthew 18:33). The Lord gives us every opportunity to walk in love by forgiving others as He has forgiven us. If we continue to refuse to forgive, the Heavenly Father will not forgive us. To forgive is to be forgiven. Our prayers and pleas will go unanswered if we do not forgive and we cannot afford to have our prayers go unanswered. *"When you stand to pray, if you have anything against anyone, forgive him that your Father in heaven may also forgive you"* (Mark 11:25). There remains no excuse for a Christian not to forgive when they have been recipients of forgiveness through God's grace that permeates with love. Can you separate love from forgiveness? If you love from the heart, forgiveness will follow.

The Lord's prayer says, *"… forgive us our debts as we forgive our debtors …"* (Matt. 5:12). We are praying to be forgiven in the proportion we forgive. Jesus summed it up when He said, *"If you forgive men their trespasses, your heavenly Father will also forgive you. But if you do not forgive …. neither will your Father forgive your trespasses"* (Matt. 5:14-15). Not to forgive is to repay evil for evil and not have regard for the good thing forgiveness does. It glorifies God through sacrificially loving in the midst of injustice. Isn't that what Jesus did for us? He loved us in the midst of our wrongdoings and had compassion on us, *"for by grace we are saved"* (Eph. 2:5).

Love always costs us something, especially if the love is

sincerely from the heart. There will be times when we will have to swallow our pride and extend to someone the same love and forgiveness we were freely given. To be overcome by evil is to withhold forgiveness from those who have wronged you, spoken evil of you, harmed you, or stolen from you, but you can overcome evil with the good of forgiveness. When I forgave those who abused and abandoned me as a child, those who spoke evil of me, those who discriminated against me, those who persecuted me, those who disobeyed me, and those who hated me, I freed myself from the torture associated with unforgiveness. No longer did I have to replay the memories that tortured me; I could renew my mind by choosing to forgive and this put me in the position to be healed of my pain. Although I have historical memories of the wrongs, I no longer have the pain because I released it to the Lord and He taught me how to love the pain away. To walk in love is a choice, a personal choice. You have to choose whether you want to continue being tormented, or whether you have had enough and decided to love by forgiving. Freedom is in your court. Choose today to walk in love and forget silly offenses that hinder you from loving others as Christ has loved you. We all make mistakes, so don't punish yourself, or dwell on condemning thoughts. Know that God's love does not condemn you; you have an advocate with the Father, Jesus Christ, and the Holy Spirit is always interceding for us when we do not know what to pray (Romans 8:26-27). You are covered with love when you confess your sins and walk in love. When you and I choose to love those who hurt us, we send up a sweet aroma to God, our Father.

THE LION'S ROAR

"Will a lion roar in the forest when He has no prey?
A lion has roared! Who will not fear?" Amos 3:4, 8

Can you hear the voice of the Teacher, the Holy Spirit, saying, "Fear not!"? Fear has increased in our world and taken many victims by its roaring threats. Have you been preyed upon by the lion, the devil, who roams throughout the earth seeking to devour your faith in God with his roar? Have you fallen into a trap set by the lion to deceive you into fearing him more than God? If you have been threatened by the lion's roar, seek the truth from the Lion of Judah and live freely in Him. Listen carefully to the words of the Apostle Paul, *"Be sober, be vigilant, because your adversary the devil walks about like a roaring lion seeking whom He may devour. Resist him, steadfast in the faith"* (I Peter 5:8-9). Do not allow the devil to back you into a trap and cause you to fear, but speak the word of the Lord, knowing that greater is He who is in you than the lion's roar that is tormenting you. Refuse to be prey for the devil today and hold onto your faith in God, who is faithful even when we are faithless, because He cannot deny Himself. Live today, bold as a lion, in full assurance that the Lord is with you and that by His name you will destroy the roars of the lion. Start now by filling your mind and mouth with what the Lord says about you and refuse to be trapped by negative thoughts. If you have been victim to negativism and defeat, *"shake yourself from the dust and arise; ... loose the bonds from your neck, O captive daughter of Zion"* (Isaiah 52:2). Renew your mind with self-talk that declares your position in Christ, *"In righteousness you shall be established; you shall be far from oppression, for you shall not fear, and from terror, for it shall not come near you. No weapon formed against you shall prosper"* (Isaiah 54:14, 17).

So stop giving the devil an open door by fearing his roar. Know that the Lord is on your side and will never forsake you. Remember, Jesus' death on the cross silenced the devil so that you and I no longer have to fear him. Believe that and be at peace.

Handling Rejection

"He who hears you, hears Me, he who rejects you, rejects Me and he who rejects Me, rejects Him who sent Me." Luke 10:16

Do not be discouraged when you experience rejection from family and friends because of words you have spoken about the Lord. So often we take it personally and become offended because God's Word has been rejected. Remember, we did the same thing to those who proclaimed the Word to us when we were not walking with Christ. *"You He made alive, who were dead in trespasses and sins, in which you once walked according to the course of this world, according to the prince of the power of the air, the spirit who now works in the sons of disobedience, among whom also we all once conducted ourselves in the lusts of our flesh, fulfilling the desires of the flesh and of the mind, and were my nature children of wrath, just as the others"* (Eph. 2:1-3). This life is not about us! This life is not about being free of hardships, persecution, and trials. Let God use your trials for His glory and your maturity; *"In this you greatly rejoice, though now for a little while, if need be, you have been grieved by various trials, that the genuineness of your faith, being much more precious than gold that perishes, though it is tested by fire, may be found to praise, honor and glory at the revelation of Jesus Christ"* (I Peter 1:7). Believe that the ministry of proclaiming God's Word is not about us, but about God's will being done. Remember, Jonah got puffed up and annoyed when God did not judge the people of Nineveh. He was more concerned with how he looked before them than seeing God's compassion and mercy touch their lost souls. He acted like we do when the Lord gives us judgments to speak to someone to correct their ways, but does not carry out those judgments because the people chose to turn from their evil ways. Like Jonah, you do not like to look like a fool, but if your ministry is not about your glory, you would not be upset when people reject what you say. Jesus said that if we follow Him, we will suffer persecution, rejection, and hatred. If we believe that Jesus is in us to save the lost, we should preach the Word in and out of season. If we believe Jesus is with us, we will rejoice when people reject us, knowing that Christ suffered likewise. *"He is despised and rejected by men, a man of sorrows and acquainted with grief and we hid, as it were, our faces from Him"* (Isaiah 53:3). In John 6:60-66, Jesus experienced rejection from many of His followers because they could not understand that He was the bread of eternal life that came down from Heaven. As it is written and quoted by Jesus, *"Man shall not live by bread alone, but by every word that proceeds from the mouth of God"* (Matt. 4:4). So, when you suffer rejection, meditate on these words, *"Blessed are you when men hate you and when they exclude you ... Rejoice and be exceedingly glad for great is your reward in Heaven, for so persecuted the prophets who were before you"* (Matt. 5:11; Luke 6:22-23). Remember, in this world we will suffer rejection. Focus not on your emotions, but Jesus Christ, whose peace will calm your emotions. Believe in His presence and be fully persuaded that He is a friend that sticks closer than a brother (Proverb 18:24). He is with you even when everyone seems to have abandoned you. So, rejoice my sister and brother, in the truth that you are not abandoned by the only One whose presence matters. *"God is our refuge and strength, a very present help in trouble. Therefore, we will not fear"* (Psalm 46:1-2).

MORE THAN CONQUERORS!

*"What shall we say to these things? If God is for us,
who can be against us?"* Romans 8:31

When all around you seems to be falling apart and the
dictates of your mind and body are yelling defeat, know
that the truth will free you to cast down these imaginations at
the feet of Jesus Christ. Do not listen to thoughts that speak the
opposite of what God's Word says. When you have pursued an
employment opportunity that seemed to be going in your favor
and then fell through, the devil will seek to consume you with
a spirit of defeat. He prowls to and fro, throughout the earth,
looking for prey to devour and rob of the benefits of the Word
of God. In Jesus' parable of the seed and the soils, He said,
*"When they hear, Satan comes immediately and takes away the word
that was sown in their hearts"* (Mark 4:15). Luke said, *"Those by
the wayside are the ones who hear; then the devil comes and takes
away the word out of their hearts, lest they should believe and be
saved"* (Luke 8:12). Wow! The truth is revealed, and the verdict
is in on Satan's schemes and tricks. He wants to steal the Word
of God that we hear before it reaches our hearts and takes root
because He knows it will save us from his attacks. It is vital that
we guard our hearts from the lies of Satan and hold onto the
beginning of our confidence until we receive the fulfillment of
God's promise. Do not listen to the liar and accept his defeat,
but remember what the Apostle Paul said, *"In all these things
we are more than conquerors through Him who loved us"* (Rom.
8:37). No weapon of Satan can prosper against us unless we let

them. If God is on our side and is mindful of us, how can we be defeated? If God did not spare His own Son, will He not freely give us the things that promote His plan for our lives? So, my beloved brethren, be encouraged that you are more than a conqueror. No weapon can prosper against you if you believe the Lord is guiding the affairs and events of your life. I believe everything is working out for our good when doors that were opened suddenly close. The Lord is saying, "... *know that all things work together for good to those who love God, to those who are called according to His purpose*" (Rom. 8:28). Be encouraged that the Lord knows the plans He has for your life, "*I will visit you and perform My good word toward you ... I know the thoughts that I think toward you, says the Lord, thoughts of good, not of evil, to give you a future and a hope. Then you will call upon Me and go and pray to Me and I will listen to you. And you will seek Me and find Me, when you search for Me with all your heart. I will be found by you says the Lord*" (Jer. 29:10-14). Remember that you prayed and sought the Lord about the job opportunity and asked that He close the door if it wasn't the door He wanted you to walk through. He answered your prayers according to His plans for your life, so resist feeling defeated and discouraged, as if the Lord has abandoned you. Rejoice that your prayers were heard and answered. Remember the word of the Lord to Joshua, "... *only be strong and very courageous ... this book of the Law shall not depart out of your mouth, but you shall meditate in it day and night that you may do according to all that is written in it. For then you will make your way prosperous and then you will have good success. Have I not commanded you? Be strong and of good courage, do not be afraid, nor be dismayed, for the Lord your God is with you wherever you go*" (Joshua 1:6-9). How can you and I fail when the Lord is with us? His very presence makes us more than conquerors because "*He who is in you is greater than He* [the devil] *who is in the world"* (I John 4:4). We have been empowered with His Holy Spirit of Jesus Christ, our Lord, who won the victory and made us more than conquerors. So, resist the devil's lies today and walk by faith and not by sight. Allow the truth of God's Word to free you from Satan's lies that closed doors equal defeat. Speak the Word to your soul and go in the peace of God knowing that the battle has been won. *"Examine yourself as to whether you are in the faith. Test yourself. Do you not know yourself, that Jesus Christ is in you?"* (II Cor. 13:5). *"We have this treasure in earthen vessels that the excellence of the power may be of God and not of us"* (II Cor. 4:7). We have an excellent power in us to handle anything the enemy throws at us today. We have the power of the Conqueror in us, so go in the Spirit of the Conqueror and be more than a conqueror. To God be the glory!

STUCK ON PAUSE?

"Behold, I will do a new thing, now it shall spring forth; shall you not know it?" Isaiah 43:19

Tired of the same old humdrum? Do you feel life is passing you by while you are stuck on pause? You wake up each morning and feel like you are the leading star in the Ground Hog Day movie, experiencing the same things over and over to the point of drudgery and boredom. Is your job a source of drudgery? Do you feel a lack of enthusiasm toward each new day? Are you confused about your purpose in life? Have you lost the joy that once filled your heart? If any of these questions resemble what you are feeling or thinking today, be encouraged, change is on the way. You are in a good position for God to show up with a new thing and fire up your passion for life. I know because I have been released from self-made prisons that tortured me with the fear to give up my God-given visions and dreams. Like you, I was stuck on pause so long that the "play" function stopped working. I stopped living with expectancy for God to show up each day with a miracle, and I started expecting a repeat of yesterday, as if my life was being controlled like a media or DVR player. When I remembered the words of the Lord, that He was calling forth a new thing into my life, hope returned and renewed my ability to believe that God is able to make my dreams come true. He declared in His word that something new is about to spring forth. He is a God that quickens the dead and calls things that are not in existence—to resurrect dead dreams. Speak the Word of God to your dreams and see them take on new life. Paul said that if we confess with our mouth God's Word, we will be delivered. Do you need deliverance? What did you dream of becoming when you were a child? Did you dream of owning your own business, to write motivational publications, to become an artist, a teacher, a preacher, a mother, an interior or fashion designer, or buyer for a large store chain? Just know that everyone has dreams, whether spoken or in secret. Maybe it's time to renew your mind and prove what is the acceptable and perfect will of God for your life. Maybe it's time to embrace Springtime, when new blossoms surface after a dead and cold season. Give the old, dead season to the Lord because it is over, never to appear again. Listen to what Paul said in II Corinthians 15: 17, *"If anyone is in Christ, He is a new creation, old things have passed away, behold all things have become new .... all things are of God."* God is behind the scenes creating something new, a new season for your life, a new chapter, a renewed dream. Spring is in bloom! All you have to do is believe and embrace the new season by faith. Go ahead and press the "play" button and release those dreams that have been stuck on "pause" and activate your dreams again. As the lyrics to the gospel song of Israel Houghton say, "It's a new season, it's a new day." Sing these lyrics over your life each day and take a deep breath of faith and watch God move. Remember this truth, *"The word is near you, in your mouth and in your heart, that is the word of faith"* (Romans 10:8). Start proclaiming the truth of God's Word to your heart and see how the power of God will make a road in the wilderness of your life. Nothing is impossible with God if you believe He can perform the impossible. His arms are not too short that He cannot reach down into your heart and resurrect your dreams to use your God-given abilities to their full potential. I had a philosophy professor tell me that I wrote like a poet and that I should not allow my stories to die in me. He encouraged me to continue writing, but I pushed the pause button and stopped writing for more than a decade. Now that a new season has come, I am enthusiastic each time that I can turn on my computer and write the words God has poured into my heart—as I am doing now. A new freedom comes when you embrace God's call upon your life with the faith that He will perform the good work He has begun. Start believing the words in Jeremiah 29:11: *"I know the thoughts that I think toward you, says the Lord, thoughts of peace and not of evil, to give you a future and a hope."* Get in gear with God and cast down every imagination that works against the dreams God gave you. Know that the Lord is mindful of you and that He is working behind the scenes, creating a new season, a new day for you to proclaim that the Dream Maker resurrects dead dreams and makes them come true for those who believe in Him.

MADE FOR REJOICING

"This is the day that the Lord has made; let us rejoice and be glad in it." Psalm 118:24

Why are you so unhappy when you wake up? The Psalmist said in Psalm 30:5, *"Sorrow is only for a night, but joy comes every morning."* It is time to end all the dreading of the day because of all the activities that sometimes cause anxiety and approach the day with rejoicing. Paul said, *"Rejoice in the Lord always, again, I say rejoice!"* (Phil. 4:4). This is an attitude of the heart, not an emotion generated by something external. We can rejoice because the Lord's Spirit dwells in us and His fruit is joy unspeakable. *"The fruit of the Spirit is love, joy, peace …,"* (Gal. 3:23) not the dread of facing another day. Where the Holy Spirit of God is, there is liberty to rejoice in God's goodness that has been bestowed upon us each day. David says the Lord daily loads us with benefits. Paul said, *"Every good gift and every perfect gift is from above and comes down from the Father of lights"* (James 1:17). We are a blessed people and have no justification for holding onto a dreadful attitude that only seeks to steal our joy. This day was made by God for rejoicing because He is with us, never to abandon us. *"The Lord is with us as a mighty awesome One"* (Jer. 20:11). The preacher said, *"nothing is better for a man than that He should eat and drink and that His soul should enjoy the good of His labor. This also, I saw was from the hand of God … for God gives joy to a man who is good in His sight"* (Ecc. 3:24-26). If the Lord has allowed you to wake up and see this new day, you have the responsibility to give Him thanks by embracing an attitude of joy. For too long you and I have allowed our To-Do lists to burden us and leave us with dreadful attitudes, where joy toward being alive no longer exists. But, let your life undergo a threat, such as a heart attack or near fatal accident, and it will take on new meaning. When I was released from the hospital's cardiac care unit it was a joy just to be alive. I remember being filled with thanksgiving for receiving another chance at living life with joy and gladness in my heart because He has been so good to me. Listen carefully to the wise message from Ecclesiastes: Rejoice and be glad to have life and strength to enjoy the works of our hands because they are from God. Many have labored to achieve and succeed in life only to find out that at the day of one's death someone else will reap the benefits of your labor. They will enjoy what you have spent your life working hard to accomplish and they may not appreciate how hard you worked. So, why not be the one to enjoy all the works of your hands while you have life today. If you don't, be assured that someone else will. If you are a homemaker, enjoy your home. If you are an artist, enjoy creating. If you love cooking, enjoy cooking for others. If you are a parent, enjoy your children while they are under your wings and pass onto them the joy of life. If you are a spouse, enjoy your mate, because death will come, and it will be too late to enjoy each other. If you are a gardener, enjoy the moments playing and planting in the soil. *"Nothing is better for a man than that he should eat and drink, and that his soul should enjoy good in his labor. This also, I saw, was from the hand of God"* (Eccles. 2:24). The bottom line is this: Life on earth, as we know it, will come to an end. We must seize each day and rejoice and be glad for all God has given us. Joy is a choice! Choose to let the Holy Spirit spring up within you the living waters of joy because God has been good to you. He has enabled you to live to see this day that was made for rejoicing. This is the day the Lord has made, so rejoice that God is with you, working in you His good pleasure. Embrace joy today!

WATCH AND WAIT!!

"I will stand my watch and watch to see what He will say to me." Habakkuk 2:2

"Wait on the Lord; Be of good courage and He shall strengthen your heart; Wait, I say on the Lord!" Psalm 27:14

What does it take for you to stand or sit still until the Lord speaks to you and answers whatever question you have? Why is waiting so difficult? Why are you so anxious and troubled about so many things when you cannot add one minute to your life or keep your hair from turning gray? In all of our lives, there is a time to wait and be patient, having confidence in God's faithfulness to speak in His timing. Waiting is a struggle and a shortcoming for many and our actions reveal this truth. We honk the horn when the driver in front of us does not move immediately when the traffic light changes. When we travel on the highways and get behind "slow" drivers who are doing the speed limit, we are quick to become irritated. Road rage has become the outcome of our impatience and poor self-control. Why are we so impatient? Has your impatience spilled over into your relationship with the Lord? Do you expect your prayers to be answered the moment they are uttered? We often expect instant replies from the Lord. This is dangerous because it jeopardizes our relationship with the Lord and opens the door to sin. Proverbs 19:2 says "He sins who hastens with His feet." God is never in a hurry and He does not want us to live a hurried lifestyle. It causes us to think that if we rush we can make things happen according to our timetable. If we rush, we are not trusting God to supply our needs. If we take matters into our hands, we open ourselves up to self-imposed sufferings. Maybe He did not want you to go to the mission field at the time you went, maybe He did not want you to marry the one you chose, maybe He did not want you to buy the house or car because He knew the economy would fall, or maybe He did not want you to take the first job offered to you because He had a better one waiting. Failing to wait on the Lord can lessen, delay, or deprive us of God's best. But if we wait, He will show up and fulfill His promises to us. He is faithful to His Word and honors the petitions of those who wait in confidence and faith that the Lord will perform all that concerns us, even if we are running late for an appointment. I have seen the intervention of the Lord when the clock seemed to drive me to take matters into my own hands and rush to an appointment or event. One morning I awakened a little late to take my husband to catch the Metro to work. I called out to Him and asked if He knew what time it was. He did not realize how little time He had left to shower and dress. I jumped out of bed, quickly dressed, and ran downstairs to prepare him some breakfast to have on the train. During all the meal preparation, I was constantly tempted to rush him to get ready as fast as possible. Instead of yielding to these impulses, I kept my mouth shut and focused on this word from the Lord; *"Be anxious for nothing, but in everything by prayer and supplication, with thanksgiving, let your requests be made known to God"* (Phil. 4:6). He would get us to the train on time. This did not lessen the attacking thoughts when we got in the car ten minutes later than we should have with a thirty-minute drive ahead of us, but I held on to the word that my timelines are in the Lord's hands and He will perform all the things that concern me. I resisted the temptation to speed and instead focused on making the time we had meaningful and pleasant. I kept casting down thoughts to maneuver around slower cars and, instead, recited over and over, "My times are in Your hand." "The Lord will perfect that which concerns me" (Psalm 138:8). You know what time the train comes and the time my husband needs to be on board." We arrived at the train station with ten minutes to spare to sit and talk. The Lord's intervention took the ten minutes that we were behind schedule and made it work for us, to our benefit. It is so important that we learn to be patient and wait on the Lord's help during times of need. Stop all the rushing and hurrying! It reveals that you are not trusting in the Lord, but are leaning on your own understanding. If you are seeking guidance and direction for today, discipline yourself to wait on the Lord. Develop strategies to overcome impulses to take the controls from God. He will answer in His timing. If you are called to write a book, or minister as a teacher, wait on the Lord to open the needed doors or part the necessary waters. Adopt the attitude of Habakkuk and take your stand at the doorpost of the Lord's house and declare; "*I will stand my watch ...*" (Habak. 2:1) and watch to see what the Lord will say to me of what He wants me to do. His vision for my life is for an appointed time and I will wait for it to come to pass, knowing that the Lord will complete what He began in me. I will declare the same faith of Abraham and not waver when it comes to the promises of God. I will give glory to God when all around me beckons me to rush, nag, take charge, express rage, or get even. God is able to perform what He promised and all we have to do is trust in Him to get us where we need to be. Do as King David did, "*I will cry out to God Most High, To God who performs all things for me*" (Psalm 57:2). "*Whenever*

I am afraid, I will trust in You" (Psalm 56:3). *"Those who wait on the Lord shall renew their strength ..."* (Isa. 40:31). It is better to trust in the Lord than to put confidence in man (human beings, yourself). *"The Lord will perfect that which concerns me ..."* (Psalm 138:8). *"Whatever the Lord pleases He does ..."* (Psalm 135:6). Today, when you hear His voice guiding you, do not harden your heart by ignoring Him. The Lord longs for His people to listen to Him and receive His blessings. *"Oh, that My people would listen to Me ..."* (Psalm 81:13). No matter what you are going through, wait on the Lord and He will carry you through it even if He has to lift you up on eagle's wings. Just know that waiting on Him pays off more than taking matters into your own hands by rushing to make things happen. Wait and be of good courage, God is faithful!

BE CONFIDENT!

"Do not cast away your confidence which has great reward. You have need of endurance, so that after you have done the will of God, you may receive the promise." Hebrews 10:35-36

Where is your confidence? In what are you confident? In whom do you turn to when needs arise? Why are you so discouraged and troubled in heart when trials come upon you? Have you been listening to those who say, *"Do not pray for patience, if you do, you will receive opportunities to be patient?"* Have you thrown away your confidence in God because He has allowed you to suffer and has not answered your prayers? These are questions I had to ask myself during a time of struggle. One morning, as I opened my Bible to spend a quiet moment with God, in my heart I knew it was the right thing to do even though I had a list of pressing errands to run. I needed to set my mind on Him so I could know His will for me that day. I found several verses that touched my spirit and challenged me to review who or what I was putting my confidence in. When I think of those who have shared their struggles with me, I find that insecurity was a common issue. We lose confidence in God's promises when we are impatient and afraid of missing out. Yet, God's Word continually reminds us not to lose confidence in Him, but to hold onto His word until our prayers are answered, even if it takes years. It took more than thirty years to see salvation for many loved ones. My mother accepted Christ one month before she died. A sister accepted Christ after thirty years of lifting her up before the Lord. Two brothers accepted Christ before they died in their 50s. I am still waiting for other relatives to come to know the saving grace of our Lord and Savior. I am holding onto God's promise in Acts 16:31: *"Believe on the Lord Jesus Christ and you will be saved, you and your household."* I have confidence in God's Word that He is not willing that any of my loved ones should die in their sins. Too often we give up because our levels of endurance are low and we don't persevere. Paul encourages us to trust that God is still performing a work in you and me. Listen to what he says: *"Being confident of this very thing, that He who has begun a good work in you will complete it until the day of Jesus Christ,"* (Phil. 1:6). We need self-discipline in waiting on the Lord. We are warned not to put confidence in our flesh, because it will only discourage us when emotions and feelings change (Phil. 3:3). When you pray to God and He does not respond according to your timetable, be on the alert for restlessness, anxiety, and discouragement to swell up like a flood. If you put your confidence in the Lord, you will receive a reward. *"Now this is the confidence that we have in Him, that if we ask anything according to His will, He hears us. And if we know* [are confident] *that He hears us, whatever we ask, we know* [are confident] *that we have the petitions that we asked of Him"* (I John 5:14-15). If your confidence is not in the Lord, do not expect anything from Him. For *"without faith it is impossible to please Him, for he who comes to God must believe that He is, and that He is a rewarder of those who diligently seek Him"* (Heb. 11:6). You will not receive anything from the Lord if you do not have confidence in Him as your Father, Provider, Healer, Guide, Strength, Peace, Joy, Promoter, Friend, and Helper. I have learned that *"it is better to trust in the Lord than to put confidence in man"* (Psalm 118:8). He knows what is best for us all. So, today, if you hear His voice saying, "Put your hope in God!" Resist all forms of doubt and unbelief that comes to break your confidence. Be encouraged by the words about Abraham's attitude toward God's faithfulness, *"He did not waver at the promise of God through unbelief, but was strengthened in faith, giving glory to God, and being fully convinced that what He had promised He was also able to perform"* (Rom. 4:20-21). Hold onto your confidence and hope firmly to the end. The confidence you had in the Lord at the beginning of your relationship with Him has great rewards (Heb. 3:6, 14). Endeavor to put your confidence in the Lord today no matter what you feel, see, or hear, for this is what perseverance is about.

GOD HAS NOT QUIT WORKING

"Being confident of this very thing, that He who begun a good work in you will complete it until the day of Jesus Christ" Philippians 1:6

When thoughts of discouragement cloud your mind and make you feel as if something is missing in your life, or that you are not fulfilling your destiny, know that God has not quit working. Although everything around you says that God has forgotten you, He hasn't and won't! Know and trust the truth of God's Word, *"... for it is God who works in you both to will and to do for His good pleasure"* (Phil. 2:13). He is still working on you and me until His plans for our lives are fulfilled. He said, *"I know the thoughts that I think toward you, says the Lord, thoughts of peace not evil, to give you a future and a hope"* (Jer. 29:11). The Lord's plans for our lives are to give us futures filled with hope that comes from seeking and searching for Him with all our hearts. You must put complete trust in the Lord and not listen or lean on your own doubtful understanding. He is working in you what is well pleasing in His sight (Heb. 13:21). Do not be afraid of missing the path your life was created to travel on. Be encouraged during the times when it seems like you are not doing anything significant for others. Perhaps you are in a season in which the Lord God is preparing your heart for a future work. If so, wait on the Lord with courage. Cast down every imagination that discourages you or breeds fear. The work the Lord is performing in you is not dependent upon human might and power. Until we learn to abide and rest in the Lord at all times, our success will be hindered. Jesus said, *"I am the vine, you are the branches. He who abides in Me, and I in Him, bears much fruit; for without Me you can do nothing"* (John 15:5). Do not be deceived into thinking that you determine your destiny and, therefore, you must maintain full control. The truth is the Lord wants the controls of your life, that He may perform the work He began the day you invited Him to dwell in your heart. He wants us to realize what the Apostle Paul realized, *"Not that we are sufficient of ourselves to think of anything as being from ourselves, our sufficiency is from God who also made us sufficient as ministers … not of the letter but of the Spirit* (II Cor. 3:5-6). Paul makes it clear that it is through the power of the Holy Spirit that He is able to perform the work God planned for His life. The same is true for Christians; we cannot do God's work without God. Only God can make us adequate enough to accomplish the work He created us to do. We are not sufficient in ourselves, nor do we have the power to carry out the Lord's will apart from abiding and trusting in Him. It is time to cast all anxieties about your destiny upon the Lord and let God work in you His will. Remember, *"Not by might nor by power, but by My Spirit; Says the Lord"* (Zech. 4:6). Sing the song, "He's still working on me to make me what I ought to be."

WHOM SHALL I FEAR?

"This I know, because God is for me. ... I will not be afraid. What can man do to me?" Psalm 56:9b, 11b

Why is there so much fear running rampant in this world? Why do we spend our hard-earned money and physical strength on fear? We have paid to be frightened when we see horror movies and TV that pumps heavy doses of fear into our homes. News shows are one of the major sources of fear-filled messages of killers, rapists, robbers, threatening storms, viruses, and scams. Some information provides necessary warnings, but how do we keep from fearing these things that torment us? How do we control what we think or speak? The first approach to take is to put your trust in the power of God whenever fear comes knocking on your door. King David promoted this when He said, *"Whenever I am afraid, I will trust in You. ... In God I have put my trust; I will not fear. What can [anyone] do to me? ...When my heart is overwhelmed; Lead me to the rock that is higher than I. The Lord is on my side. I will not fear. What can man do to me? It is better to trust in the Lord Than to put confidence in man"* (Psalm 56:3-4; 61:2b; 118:6, 8). The Lord, who has all power in His hands, will be a strong tower, a hiding place, a refuge for anyone who puts their trust in Him, but you have to make that choice. Who will you trust when fear knocks on the door of your heart? Will you follow David's example and call on the Lord? He is the only trustworthy source in times of fear. The Psalms are replete with examples of David battling his fears. His words can help you overcome your tormenting fears that keep you from enjoying God's peace. We are encouraged to trust in the Lord with all of our hearts, at all times, even when we are crying for help. *"Trust in Him at all times, you people; Pour out your heart before Him; God is a refuge for us"* (Psalm 62:8). Further encouragement comes from the words of Jesus, "... *do not fear those who kill the body but cannot kill the soul. But rather fear Him who is able to destroy both soul and body in hell ... Do not fear therefore; you are of more value than many sparrows"* (Matt. 10:28, 31). If God loves us enough to number the hairs on our head, surely He will protect who He counts as precious in His sight—you and me! Fearing continuously will only weaken your faith and give you what you feared. Job proved that what we fear in our hearts will come to pass if we focus on our fears. Remember, *"Faith is the substance of things hoped for and the evidence of things not seen"* (Heb. 11:1). Listen to what Job said; *"For the thing I greatly feared has come upon me, and what I dreaded has happened to me"* (Job 3:25). Fear will destroy what God meant for good if you let it. The choice is yours. No one can break down the protective hedge God's presence has placed around you but you, by the words you affirm. If you speak the Word of God when fear comes knocking, God's power will deliver you from all your fears. Know the truth and be confident that God's Word will work on your behalf. David said in Psalm 118:6, *"This I know, because God is for me .... I will not be afraid. What can man do to me?"* Declare God's presence in your life. Speak to your fears and say, "The Lord is with me, I will not fear anyone or anything because the Lord is my strong tower in which I run into Him and find safety. He is the rock that I can stand on when fears overwhelm me. Although you may cry sometimes, cry to the Lord and seek His deliverance from all your fears because all power belongs to Him. Speak this:

"Get behind me fear, for it is written," "*Only fear the Lord* ..." (I Sam. 12:24a).

Speaking God's Words will encourage and empower us to stop fear in its tracks and limit its power over our lives. We must allow only the messages that keep us in the faith to reside in our minds. Know this, you make the choice today whether to be tormented by fear or live by faith in God. Today, God has set before all of us choices that bring life or death, blessings or curses. Fear steals peace, but faith produces a love for God that comes from obeying His command: Fear not!

Having God In The Boat

"Why are you so fearful? How is it that you have no faith?" Mark 4:40

As the disciples of Christ used boats to get them where they wanted to go, we have vehicles that move us from one place to another. We never anticipate sudden storms coming up to threaten us and make our journeys seem impossible. The disciples did not anticipate life-threatening waves to interrupt their journey to the other side, nor did they realize who was in the boat with them. The same heart attitude is true for you and me when we are consumed with fear because of the threatening sights that disrupt our journeys. Sadly, we let fear drown out our faith because we walk by sight. This was my experience the first time I went white water rafting with my family. I was still dreading the thought of snakes along the shoreline and rocks that could hurt me and contemplating returning to the tour bus when I found myself hurrying into our raft. It all happened so quickly that before I knew it, I was in the boat in rushing waters that seemed to be moving 100 miles per hour. I was determined not to pop out of the raft, so I tightened my grip on the handles as if my life depended on them. My family tried to encourage me to look up and enjoy the beauty of the surroundings, but I was so frightened I could only see the blurring speed of the water. The fear on my face caused my family more concern than it did me, being that this was their first time rafting too. Why was I so fearful when I was in the boat with those I love and who loved me? There was an invisible tourist in the boat with us, but I did not turn my thoughts toward Him until near the end of the rafting trip down Snow Mass Mountain. I could hear echoes in my ears saying, *"Fear not, I am with you"* (Isaiah 41:10). I slowly lifted my head and captured the beautiful landscape of trees, bridges, and homes along the shoreline. I began to loosen my grip on the raft handles as I switched from listening to fear to listening to the words of the Apostle Paul, *"For God has not given us a spirit of fear, but of power and of love and of a sound mind"* (II Tim. 1:7). Fear torments and keeps you from seeing the invisible presence of the Lord. I was blinded, but thank God for sufficient grace that kept me from totally missing out on this wonderful adventure and the joy of being with my family. Whether you are in a raft, car, bus, train, airplane, boat, or ship, know that you are not alone should a storm suddenly arise. Storms will come our way, but we must keep our eyes fixed on Jesus, the Author and Finisher of our faith. He is the only One who can speak to the storms and calm their destructive forces. Having the Lord, in your boat means that it will be well with your soul, so there is no need to be afraid or to tighten your grip. Boldly say, *"The Lord is my helper, I will not fear"* (Heb. 13:6). *"For I the Lord will hold your right hand, saying to you, 'Fear not', I will help you"* (Isaiah 41:13). When we fear not reaching our destination in life or that our journey will be disrupted by health or financial storms, we must remember who is in the boat with us. He promised never to leave or forsake us. There is no storm in this life that can separate you from the love of God that is in Christ Jesus. He will carry you safely to your destination if you believe He is with you.

PRESS ON!

"... I press on ... forgetting what lies behind and reaching forward to what lies ahead. I press on toward the goal for the prize of the upward call of God in Christ Jesus." Philippians 3:12-13 NASB

D o you feel hemmed in by the past? Are old experiences preventing you from moving forward into a new beginning? Have you been living on the blessings and joys of the past because no new blessings or miracles have come your way for a long time? Maybe it is because you have not fully embraced each new day with the expectation that God will load you with new blessings. Sometimes we get stuck on past blessings and limit God from doing something new. The words of the Apostle Paul opened my blind eyes and I pray yours are opened too. It is time to put the old blessings of opportunities, provisions, healings, and guidance away in a book of remembrance and start believing the Lord to open new doors, provide new provision, new healings, and give new guidance. Think about it, would you eat a meal that was prepared for you last year? Would you drink water that had sat on your nightstand for two years? No! You would seek fresh food and water each day. Why not apply this truth to the things you need in your life today? Allow the Lord to give you fresh spirit food and drink from His Word so you can press on into the future He has planned for you. Embrace this new day, a day that has never been before, and forget yesterday, because it is gone forever. Whatever you did not accomplish yesterday can never be moved into a new day because no one can turn back the clock. We cannot travel back in time and correct our mistakes or take advantage of missed opportunities. Our lives were created to move forward, not backwards. According to Isaiah 43:18, God is about to do a new thing when the past in put where it belongs, in the past: "Do not remember the former things or consider the things of old. I am about to do a new thing; now it shall spring forth, do you not perceive it?" (Isaiah 43:18-21) This is a new day in which your faith is the like paint on the brush of an artist who can paint a new picture for your life today. God is the artist of our lives when we turn our lives over to Him and declare with King David, *"This is the day the Lord has made"* (Psalm 118:24). Look! The word of the Lord through the mouth of Paul declares that we are new creations each day and the old has passed away. Embrace today as the best day of your life and live it filled with faith that nothing is impossible with God. He is able to move you forward to reach and achieve your goal to become what He called you to become in this season of your life. Expect new miracles, new blessings, new provisions, new directions, and new opportunities to fill your life with new joy. Press onward into the newness of life and see the new thing God has prepared for you.

A Servant's Attitude

"Make a joyful noise unto the Lord ... Serve the Lord with gladness, come before His presence with singing." Psalm 100:1-2 KJV

Have you lost your joy in serving others? Do you feel like you are always serving alone while others sit at the table waiting to receive the benefits of your service? Do you put much time and effort into making life comfortable for others at the sacrifice of your own comfort? As the years go by do you find that your joy toward serving has been replaced by a resentful and begrudging attitude toward anyone who requests your time? Do you no longer look forward to or welcome the opportunity to serve the needs of others because your needs have been neglected for so long. If you have found yourself entertaining any of these attitudes toward serving, you have lost focus on who you really are serving. You have taken a detour from the way the Lord ordained you to serve, with joy and gladness of heart. It is time to get back on the path that is highlighted by the word of the Lord. If you return to rejoicing in the Lord for the abundance of all things and do as Paul advised, "rejoice in the Lord always, again I say rejoice," (Phil. 4:4) the joy of the Lord will swell up in you like rivers of living water. Ever wonder why you have felt so fatigued and overwhelmed before preparing to serve? Perhaps you have not allowed the joy of the Lord to be your strength because you have not fully cast [thrown] all your cares and anxieties of the event on Him in prayer and thanksgiving. Prayer does change things.

It will change your attitude from giving service begrudgingly to cheerful giving as unto the Lord and not to people. Our attitude affects everything we do. I have experienced times when my attitude became embittered toward giving my home to host others because of overwhelming thoughts of all the serving that was required. All the meals to prepare, cleaning before and after guests arrive, and shopping to meet their nutritional needs have consumed most of the day and sent me to bed a weary and unhappy camper. Any offered help was toward the end of the task. I had become critical and judgmental toward those I served when they just sat without offering to help or show any consideration toward how I felt. This type of attitude has plunged me into stinking thinking as it sifted the joy of the Lord out of me and left me weak in my own strength instead of strong in the joy of the Lord. Then I returned to the Word and it gave a lamp to my feet and light to my path that I understood what I was missing. I was missing the truth that frees one to serve the Lord with gladness of heart and mind. The blessings of serving on behalf of the Lord should enrich one's life, not bring sorrow of heart. Where does the sorrow come from? It comes from leaning on your own understanding and believing that if you work hard and long hours serving in your own strength you will accomplish the tasks before you. Yes, you might succeed, but you will not have joy because you did not rely on the Lord to establish the works of your hands as you served others. You will continue to feel unfulfilled and unhappy as long as you seek to serve others without the mind of Christ controlling your attitude. We are the Lord's servants, not servants of the people in our lives. We are exhorted by Paul to remember that whatever we do, we do unto the Lord and not for people. Therefore, when people do not offer to help or express their gratitude, you are not easily offended and puffed up with resentment, but you rejoice because you served the Lord. So, go forth today and hear what the Spirit of the Lord is saying to you. Do not harden your heart by insisting on doing things your way, but seek God's will to be done. Choose to serve with joy by singing songs of thanksgiving to the Lord for all He has already done for you. Start counting your blessings and you will see how blessed you are. Joy comes whenever you recognize and count your blessings not your sorrows.

RETURN TO ME!

"Return, O backsliding children ... for I am married
unto you ... and I will heal your backslidings."
Jeremiah 3:14, 22 KJV

"Now, therefore," 'says the LORD,' "Turn to Me with
all your heart, With fasting, with weeping, and
with mourning. ... Return to the LORD your God,
For He is gracious and merciful." Joel 2:12-13

Although Jeremiah the Prophet called the children of Israel to return their hearts to the Lord God and turn from their unfaithfulness, this call seems fitting for the people of God today. If you have replaced God for the blessings of this world, you have forsaken and forgotten the Lord and played the harlot. We play the harlot whenever we go after anything other than the Lord to fulfill our needs. The tempter seduces the people of God to set their hearts on the things of this world that fulfill the lust of the flesh, the lust of the eyes, and the pride of life. The purpose of this seduction is to turn us from our forever Lord and toward the things of this temporal world. The tempter, that old Devil, is behind the scenes, getting us to worship our blessings instead of One who gave the blessings. Whenever we yield to this temptation, we are saying to the Lord, "Forget You, I have found another love that is faithful in fulfilling my cravings." As Jesus was tempted in like manner, so are we, but the difference is how we respond. Jesus spoke to the spirit behind the temptation, *"... Away with you, Satan!*

For it is written, 'You shall worship the Lord your God, and Him only you shall serve'" (Matt. 4:10). What are you worshipping and serving with your heart, soul, mind, and strength? You are serving somebody or something. Romans 6:16 says, "*… to whom you present yourselves slaves to obey, you are that one's slaves whom you obey, whether of sin leading to death, or of obedience leading to righteousness.*" We are slaves to whatever we treasure above Jesus. Jesus said that our hearts will be where our treasure is. Have you ever sat down and thought about what you treasure? Who are you really serving with your total being? Is your service an indication that God has been forgotten and removed from the picture? The same warnings given to the children of Israel should not be taken lightly by God's people today. "*Beware that you do not forget the Lord your God by not keeping His commandments … lest—when you have eaten and are full, and have built beautiful houses and dwell in them; and when … all that you have is multiplied; when your heart is lifted up, and you forget the* LORD *your God … then you say in your heart, 'My power and the might of my hand have gained me this wealth.' 'And you shall remember the* LORD *you God, for it is He who gives you power to get wealth, …*" (Deut. 8:11-14, 17-18). God is gradually replaced and forgotten when prosperity fills every area of our lives. When we need nothing from the Lord, we are in a dangerous place because He created us to be solely dependent on Him, not independent. Jesus made it clear that we cannot love and serve two masters, so we must choose who we will serve today. If you have ignored the Lord and have not been faithful in seeking first His council, guidance, and will for the days of your life, maybe you have turned your back on Him. God is gracious and merciful! He is calling His people to return to Him. Return to your first love, the One who looked beyond your faults and saw your need for a Savior. It is written in Isaiah 30:15 "In returning and rest you shall be saved." The Lord is our sufficiency in all things. He is the source of all we need to live a godly life. Apart from Him we have nothing because all the things this world offers will expire. Paul said, *"while we do not look at the things which are seen, but at the things which are not seen. For the things which are seen are temporary, but the things which are not seen are eternal"* (II Cor. 4:18). Remember, the Lord is the source for all of your needs today. Return to Him with your whole heart and let Him be the center of your life. He is always faithful, even when we are unfaithful. Look to Him today and be blessed. He misses the time you spent with Him, loving on Him with your heart, soul, mind, and strength. Take time today to remember and worship the Lord and you will resist the devil's seductive devises that cause many to go after the things this world offers. Know this, the world and all its kingdoms fulfill only the lust of the flesh, the lust of the eye, and the pride of life, all of which offer only quick fixes. Know that every person, even at their best, is but a vapor and shadow, *"they busy themselves in vain; He heaps up riches and does not know who will gather them"* (Psalm 39:4-6). If your life has been enriched with blessings, do not trust in uncertain riches, but in the living God who richly gives us all things to enjoy.

GET WISDOM!!!

"Wisdom is the principal thing. Therefore get wisdom. And in all your getting, get understanding."
Proverbs 4:7a

Wisdom cries out daily to capture our attention. How many times have we passed by wisdom to walk in ways of simplicity and complacency? Wisdom calls out to God's people at the entrances of cities and from the mountaintops. In every place that promises to give you safety and security outside of Jesus, wisdom is there crying for your attention. If we would stop and listen to what wisdom has to say, we would save ourselves much heartache and suffering. Too often we think our ways are right and the best way to obtain safety and security, but in the end, the truth hurts when we learn how foolish we were to pass by wisdom and ignore her calls. I have been a foolish woman many times when I leaned on my own understanding in pursuit of self-esteem and security. I thought that if I obtained a college education, landed an executive position with a prestigious title, lived in a prestigious neighborhood, drove a classy car, attended extravagant social functions, and traveled to exotic places, I would have guaranteed happiness. Sadly, I learned that to obtain the American dream of education, world travel, wealth, and impressive social networks only puts a bandage on the real issue. Happiness is not about what you obtain but about what obtains you. Jesus says that a person's life is not found in the abundance of earthly treasures, but in Him alone. My heart was storing up and treasuring the things the world offered that would save me from the adversities of life. The adversity of not having the symbols of success and financial security can be conquered if you get the things the world says you need to be successful. This foolish thinking based on the sensual wisdom of the world, not on the wisdom of God. In fact, I learned that the opposite is true in the pursuit of happiness and success. God requires us to listen to the counsel of His Spirit and follow the path His wisdom lays out. His wisdom instructs us to daily seek Him for wisdom in our areas of need and to trust Him for everything. The fear of the Lord is the beginning of wisdom. To humbly serve the Lord with all we have is the way of wisdom, not to seek to be served. Here's the bottom line: get wisdom and understanding by listening to and reading God's Word. If you don't know God's will for your life, pray in faith and ask for wisdom. God promises to give it generously. Remember, *"He who gets wisdom loves His own soul..."* (Prov. 19:8).

TRUST AND LEAN ON ME!

"Trust in the Lord with all your heart, And lean not on your own understanding; … Trust in Him at all times, …." Proverbs 3:5; Psalm 62:8a

Who do you rely on most? Who do you call when trouble comes in huge proportions? When the roads of life are filled with signs of detours, danger, do not enter, winding road ahead, dangerous curves, falling rocks, road blocks, work zone, stay in your lane, or check points, whom do you seek to keep you going in the right direction? Life can be a mixture of mazes of confusion to keep you from seeing a way out. But there is One who can make a crooked, curvy road straight or make a road where there is no road. If He can part a sea for His people to walk through, surely He is able to make a way for you on roads filled with obstacles. Too often we miss God's best for us because we depend and trust what we see or feel over what God is able to do. We fail to receive God's best for us because we are not totally relying on Him to make a way when we see no way. When we are hit with depression, discouragement, despair, and defeat, we become dismayed and forget who is with us. We trust the voice of our senses, or the world, or family, or friends, more than we trust the voice of the Lord God who promised never to abandon us. He sealed this promise when He sent the Holy Spirit to be with you to teach, guide, and comfort you. Do you not know that you are the temple of the Holy Spirit who lives in you and you are not left alone as an orphan? God watches over you daily. All the Lord asks is that you trust Him with your life by surrendering everything to Him: your family, your marriage, your career, your dreams, your future, and your past. Give all of yourself and your life to the Lord and trust Him to do what is best for you. When you feel confused and distracted by your own thoughts, turn these concerns over to the Lord by fixing your mind on Jesus, the author and finisher of your faith. Set your affections on things above and watch God move. Your destiny is determined by the thoughts that dominate your mind, be they negative or positive. If you want peace, try meditating on the Lord and His Word. Isaiah said that the Lord will keep in perfect peace those whose minds are stayed on Him because they trust in Him. *"Trust in the LORD forever, for in YAH, the LORD ... is everlasting strength"* (Isaiah 26:4). Even our strength to endure what life throws at us is tied to our thoughts. Paul said the God of peace will be with you if you think on things that are true, noble, just, lovely, of good report, or praiseworthy. See the Lord as your ultimate and only provider and let your actions declare that you trust in Him. He is Jehovah Jireh, the Lord who provides for us. Call on Him in your times of need, go to the throne of grace (your prayer closet), and make your requests known to Him. If He can send a raven to feed a man, put tax money in the mouth of a fish, and increase oil and meal to feed a woman and her son because she gave her last to God's servant, surely He can give you the breakthrough you have been looking for. He is faithful and will perform what He promised when faith and trust are in full control of the heart and mind of the believer and His word is the fruit that pours from their mouth. Speak His word into your obstacles and watch God make a way. Remember, you cannot complete the journey without Him. Jesus said that unless you abide in Him, you can do nothing. In Proverbs 3:7a, it says, *"Do not be wise in your own eyes,"* following the directions of your heart without inquiring of the Lord or seeking His guidance. Safety comes when we rely on the Lord for counsel on the roads ahead. Psalms 32:8 (KJV) says, *"I will instruct you and teach you the way you should go; ..."* Put your trust in the Lord today and see his salvation breakthrough on your behalf. Those who seek Him with faith and trust will not be disappointed. Paul said without faith it is impossible to please God because you must believe that He is able to provide for your needs (Heb. 11:6). Bottom line, without trusting the Lord, you limit yourself from receiving the rewards He has you. You cannot lose when your trust is in the right One. Trust in the Lord with all your heart today and refuse to follow your own understanding. The peace of God will keep your heart and mind from thoughts that disrupt and destroy your destiny.

LITTLE THINGS BIG IMPACTS

"He who is faithful in what is least is faithful also in much; and he who is unjust in what is least is unjust also in much. Better is a little with righteousness, Than vast revenues without justice. Better is little with the fear of the LORD than great treasure with trouble." Luke 16:10; Proverbs 15:16, 16:8

What is enough? How much does it take to make you content? Why do you labor daily killing yourself to accumulate provisions for today, tomorrow, and rainy days? Do you not know that what you are doing is not new because there is nothing new under the sun; someone has already walked this road before you. Look at the choices made by the children of Israel when gathering their daily provisions. God commanded them through Moses and Aaron to gather only the required quota of one Omer (9.30 cups) per person to meet their needs, but some gathered little and some more than instructed. The actions of those who gathered more made it seem as if God did not know what was enough to meet their daily needs. He was testing them to reveal what was in their hearts when it came to be fulfilling their needs. It is clear that for a piece of bread a person who is hungry will transgress because self-preservation is the law of their nature. The sad thing is that the children of Israel resemble those in the church who have gathered more than enough for themselves and have ignored the cries of the poor who beg daily for the crumbs that fall from their tables. A spirit of greed has seduced the people of God to seek self-preservation as the law to guide their lives instead of the laws of God that says, *"Give and it will be given unto you; …"* (Luke 6:38 KJV); *"Freely you have received, freely give"* (Matt. 10:8); *"He who has pity on the poor lends to the LORD, and He will reward them for what they have done"* (Prov. 19:17). *"It is more blessed to give than to receive"* (Acts 20:35). *"So let each one give as he purposes in his heart, not grudgingly or of necessity; for God loves a cheerful giver."* (II Cor. 9:7). Just the crumbs that fall from your table may be enough to make a big impact in the life of another. Do not deceive yourself into thinking you must wait until you have an abundance because you must give a lot to make a big impact. God multiplies little gifts and makes them have big impacts. As Christian Singer Danniebelle Hall said, "Little things are much when you place them in the master's hand." The miracle of Jesus' feeding the five thousand men, plus women and children, happened so we could see how little becomes big when given according to God's will. What is in your hand? How many loaves do you have? Will you be moved by compassion for those in need and share the provisions that have been given to you? I challenge you to give for the joy of giving and contentment will increase in the fragmented areas of your life. Whenever I have given talents and abilities, whether spiritual or physical, what was left over was multiplied that I had no lack. Truly, it is better to have little and use it for the glory of God than to have a lot stored up for rainy days and see it melt away. If you do not use it for God, you will lose it to the worms and it will become stinky to you. But you do not have to watch the blessings of the Lord melt away. All you have to do is turn all that you possess over to Jesus to be used as He desires, and watch your greed and discontentment melt away. As Jesus said, *"For where your treasure is, there your heart will be also. No one can serve two masters; …"* (Matthew 6:21, 24). Refuse to be a fool who builds bigger houses for all of his stuff. Recognize that all that you have has been given by God who gave you the power to obtain it. Acknowledge that the earth is the Lord's and all that is in it, including you. He created you to fulfill His plan to impact lives that are starving for the crumbs from His table. You have been blessed to have something to give to the hungry and homeless. Just open your hand wide and let the Lord show you how to reveal Him to the world. Better to give yourself and your possessions away for the Lord and see the big impact you will have in the lives of those in need around you.

MOTHER'S DAY

"… Weeping may endure for a night, But joy comes in the morning." Psalm 30:5b

Mother's Day is a day to shower mothers with symbols of appreciation for all the sacrifices they make for their families. Flowers, candy, greeting cards, meals, and specially crafted poems are gifts given to moms for jobs well done. The local merchants and media provide gift ideas for those who need help with Mother's Day. You cannot go anywhere without seeing advertisements. Your mail, email, and Internet pop-ups all bombard you with reminders that Mother's Day is coming and to be ready with the right gift in hand. Does the right gift really communicate sincere appreciation, or does it just ease the conscience of the giver? What is the right gift for the mom who has served her family at the cost of her own needs? Is any gift enough for the mom who went out of her way to let you know how special you are, when she attended all your school events, worked when her body wanted to quit so that you could attend schools that exhorted the name of Christ, worked so that you could have the wedding of your dreams, worked so that you could finish college without debt, helped you move in and paint your first home after putting in a day's work at a demanding job, and who gave you godly counsel whenever you called? What can you give a mom who seeks the Lord daily on your behalf and who has been a model of selfless service? There is no gift sufficient enough to communicate your appreciation other than what God reveals. The Lord knows the deep heart needs of every mom and He knows what is best to give her and when to give it. Seek His gift ideas and your gift will always be right and timely. He knows your mom better than you. Many children have good intentions of appreciating their moms, but often delay in carrying them out because it is not a top priority. They overlook the importance of what it means for a mom to be appreciated by her children, even if they live far away. A phone call is the quick-fix approach that involves minimum sacrifice or major effort. Sadly, honoring mom on this special day is not a priority for those who have taken her loving service for granted. But when it comes to expressing her love for her children, she becomes extravagant in showering them with tokens of love. She makes it a top priority to send greeting cards on time, to send gifts that are appropriate or the fulfillment of a desire, and makes it a point to be the first phone call greeting of the day. Distance does not change a mother's love because she fills the gaps with loving memories. She has set the pace and example for her children to follow by obeying the principle, *"Do to others as you would have them do to you"* (Luke 6:31 NIV). But for some moms the scales are not balanced by this Golden Rule and Mother's Day is a day of sorrow because they don't feel valued by their children. They called to wish her happy Mother's Day to ease their consciences, but the deeds of gift giving were as absent as their bodies. Not everyone has a good mom who was sensitive to the needs and desires. There are women who are mothers in name only and have hearts that are far from serving sacrificially for the betterment of their children. They feel like children should be indebted to them because they gave birth to them. I know because I had a mom like this who repeatedly told me that adoption was on her mind when I was born. She made little sacrifice to communicate that I was special, but I still sent her gifts and greeting cards for Mother's Day because she expected it and because I wanted to honor God by honoring my mother. I did not have to do anything to deserve God's love, so why expect my mother to do anything to deserve my love? I am glad I followed God's way until the day of my mom's death or else I would have had great regrets for putting a price tag or measurement on the amount of love my mother deserved.

Mother's Day was created to honor all mothers for giving us life. There are many of us who cannot honor our mothers because they are no longer here, but for the rest of us, take time out of your busy schedule and love her in deeds that are tailor-made for her. Your mother's needs for love are greater than you can imagine. Don't let her spend a day feeling unloved because you refuse to make her a priority. Remember all the times she showed you how special you are. Bring her joy this morning not because the masses are doing the same, but because she deserves to know you appreciate all she has sacrificed for you. Make your mom's Mother's Day a day for her to know how much she means to you.

JUDGMENT DAY

"I, the Lord, search the heart, I test the mind, Even to give every man according to His ways, According to the fruit of His doings." Jeremiah 17:10

Do not be deceived into the mindset that you can get away with doing evil things in secret. God knows where we all live. Know the truth that every knee will bow and every tongue confess that Jesus Christ is Lord. Every word we have spoken will be judged, as well as every deed, whether good or bad, for it is written, *"For we must all appear before the judgment seat of Christ, that each one may receive the things done in the body, according to what he has done, whether good or bad."* (II Cor. 5:10). Judgment day will come for everyone, so do not be fooled into thinking you can live any way you want and ignore God's presence. Live today focused on the unseen presence of the Lord and show Him the greatest amount of respect by doing good every today. Do those things that honor God and give His love to those who feel unloved; live to give to those who are hungry and thirsty, naked and homeless; live to spread hope to the hopeless, comfort to those grieving, and peace to those of troubled minds. Follow the example of Jesus and seek not to be served, but to serve and judgment day will go well for you. Periodically give yourself a spiritual self-exam, as the scriptures admonish, to see if your ways are pleasing to the Lord. Many times, I have had to examine my mouth to make sure the words that came forth were in agreement with what the Lord says I should be speaking over my life. Searching the scriptures about the mouth, I came across these verses that make it clear that judgment day was coming for the words that I have spoken, *"But I say to you that for every idle word men may speak, they will give account of it on the day of judgment. For by your words you will be justified, and by your words you will be condemned"* (Matt. 12:36-37). I was guilty of speaking what I felt for the moment, whether it was defeat, discouragement, or depression instead of declaring that I am more than a conqueror in Christ. I was reminded by the Holy Spirit that the Lord always causes those who walk by faith and not by sight (feelings) to triumph in Christ (II Cor. 2:14). I stood up and shook off these negative feelings and began to speak the positive words of Jesus over my life and my day was transformed into something joyous, instead of something dreaded. This is a daily battle we all will encounter, but we have the mighty spiritual weapons God has given us to cast down every imagination that exalts itself against what the Lord says is ours. *"Do not be rash with your mouth, And let your heart utter anything hastily before God. For God is in heaven, and you on earth; Therefore let your words be few. Do not let your mouth cause your flesh to sin, ... But fear God"* (with your mouth) Eccl. 5:2, 6a, 7b. After reading these warnings I began to pray the prayers of David, *"Create in me a clean heart, O God; Let the words of my mouth and the meditation of me heart Be acceptable in Your sight. With my mouth I will make known Your faithfulness..."* (Ps. 51:10; 19:14; 89:1b).

TRUST FUND

"Trust in the Lord with all your heart." Proverbs 3:5a

Who do you really trust? When troubles visit you, who do you seek for help? When your money runs out before the next pay period, who do you call for assistance? When gloominess clouds your mind and exhausts your enthusiasm and joy, where do you go to be uplifted and strengthened? I have witnessed intense attacks on God's people in this area of trust. Many have fallen from the faith and turned to the world for immediate relief. Payday lenders are frequent places people go to first for help in times of financial trouble. Psychiatrists and therapists are pursued for stability of mind and emotions instead of the One who created the mind. The point I am making is this: when troubles come our way, too often we seek help from what we can see, people, instead of God, who is unseen. But the Apostle Paul gave us this exhortation; *"Therefore we do not lose heart. Even though our outward man is perishing, yet the inward man is being renewed day by day. For our light affliction, which is but for a moment, is working for us a far more exceeding and eternal weight of glory, while we do not look at the things which are seen, but at the things which are not seen. For the things which are seen are temporary, but the things which are not seen are eternal"* (II Cor. 4:16-18). Resist the temptation to seek quick fixes and solutions. Do this; *"Cast your burden on the Lord, and He shall sustain* [strengthen or support mentally] *you"* (Psalm 55:22). Learn to turn all your troubles over to Jesus Christ and trust Him for everything you need. Repeat the words of King David and be encouraged and strengthened when the going gets tough; *"Whenever I am afraid, I will trust in You. In God* [I will praise His word], *In God I have put my trust; I will not fear. What can flesh do to me?"* (Psalm 56:3-4). When we do not trust the Lord, we are outside of His will and vulnerable to the enemy. The children of Israel did this when they doubted God's presence in the battle for the Promised Land; *"Then the LORD said to Moses: "How long will these people reject Me? And how long will they not believe Me, with all the signs which I have performed among them"* (Num. 14:11)? They brought on themselves the curse of defeat and failure to accomplish what God charged them to do. Joshua and Caleb tried to emphasize the importance of trusting in the Lord when they said: *"If the Lord delights in us, then He will bring us into this land and give it to us, 'a land which flows with milk and honey.' Only do not rebel against the Lord, nor fear the people of the land, for they are our bread; their protection has departed from them, and the Lord is with us. Do not fear them"* (Num. 14:8-9). Don't let hindered faith and trust rob you of the Lord's best. He is the only reliable source that will never abandon you. Surrender your heart to the Lord today, along with all the things that are causing you anxiety and stealing your inner peace. Trust in Him to be Jehovah-Jireh, your provider, and you will receive His blessings. *"Blessed is the man who trusts in the LORD, And whose hope is the Lord"* (Jer. 17:7).

People will disappoint and fail you, but the Lord will never forsake you: *"Fear not, for I am with you; Be not dismayed, for I am your God. I will strengthen you, Yes, I will help you, I will uphold you with My righteous right hand"* (Isa. 41:10). Trust Him to work all things out for your good (Rom. 8:28). He will keep you in perfect peace, free from the anxiety that produces fear when you choose to focus your mind on Him first for ALL that you need. *"You will keep in perfect peace, whose mind is stayed on You, Because he trusts in You. Trust in the Lord forever ..."* (Isaiah 26:3-4).

CALLED BY GOD!

"And the Lord called Samuel again the third time. So he arose and went to Eli and said, 'Here I am, for you did call me.' Then Eli perceived that the Lord had called the boy. Therefore Eli said to Samuel, 'Go, lie down; and it shall be, if He calls you that you must say, 'Speak, Lord, for your servant hears.'" I Samuel 3:8-9

A re you confused and frustrated to the point of despair because you do not know what the Lord has called you to do? You have prayed for years for clarity of purpose and the fog in your mind seems to have thickened as the years passed. You have taken matters into your own hands and followed the words of others because opportunity knocked on your door during your time of confusion. Like Samuel, you were more familiar with the voices of your family and friends, and you did not recognize the Lord's voice. In the darkest hours of your life, when it seemed as if the light of God's Word had gone out on the paths ahead of you, the Lord was calling you. But you must enter a season of stillness by resting in His presence until you hear His still, small voice calling your name. There is a time and season for everything and when you do not know what God has called you to do, it is time to be still and wait on God. Stop running after others' callings. Every good opportunity may not be good for you. Samuel thought Eli called Him to do something for God because Samuel did not know the word or voice of God. But you and I have no excuse.

We have so much of the word preached and sung to us that we have confused the voice of the Lord with the voice of man. I have to raise both hands in guilt because I have been confused for so long about what the Lord created and called me to do. I have followed callings of career choices that filled the voids of the moment only to find myself still wanting guidance and clarity of purpose. It seemed like whenever I became restless in waiting for an answer, I would start looking for something to do. In my heart of hearts, I know the type of positions I have worked became great distractions that dulled my spiritual ears. The demands on my time and the heavy load of responsibilities associated with these positions made sitting still before the Lord challenging. Yet, I apply for these opportunities and start crying out to the Lord again to open or close the door if this was not His will or the direction He wanted me to take. This has been a vicious cycle that I have gone around for more than a decade. I must confess that being still and quiet is a challenge for me. Not long ago I interrupted my waiting period, yet again, to seek employment, but soon my heart grew weary to the point of discouragement. Then, a breakthrough came when I heard the words of a song by Juanita Bynum, "Speak Lord, for your servant is listening." Before I knew it, I had stopped my busy work, fallen to my knees, and raised my arms high to the Lord for mercy and strength. My petition turned into begging because of my deafness to God's voice and blindness to the temptation to take the control and make things happen in my timing. The tears grew as I realized the error of my ways and how I had been praying more for myself instead of for others. I found myself praying to give up the controls over my abilities, intellect, life, and all the works of my hands, especially the things that I had been holding onto. I did not want to be in control anymore. When I rose from my knees and turned off the music, I walked around the house asking the Lord to take the controls of my life. I immediately grabbed the Bible to read the word that the Lord had guided me to over the years and my eyes were opened to the light of God's truth. I noticed written dates going as far back as 1998, notes in Jeremiah 1:4-10, with the dates of each time the Lord had lead me to this passage. I wept deeply because He had been guiding and speaking, but I had not been listening.

Many who follow the voices of the world find themselves working jobs that do not satisfy, buying stuff that leaves emptiness, and going on adventures that do not measure up to the expectations. The end result is a never-ending cycle of dissatisfaction. Until you and I do as Samuel did and determine to know whose voice we're really listening to, we will miss God's voice. Until we speak those final words, "Speak Lord, for your servant hears," we will live deaf to His will. The Lord wills that we hear what His Spirit is saying and follow His leading, no matter where it leads. Purpose to live, to listen, and to obey the voice of the Lord and proclaim the words of our Lord Jesus Christ, "... *yet not my will, but yours be done*" (Luke 22:42 NIV).

RELINQUISHING CONTROL

"I have been crucified with Christ; it is no longer I who live, but Christ lives in me …. He died for all, that those who live should no longer live for themselves, …" Gal. 2:20a; 2 Cor. 5:15a

W ho is in the control room of your life? Who is doing the driving? A long time ago, the Greyhound bus company had a jingle that went something like this, "Take Greyhound and leave the driving to us." They wanted their passengers not to worry or stress about the length of the journey or the road ahead. This is the same basic message communicated by the Apostle Paul throughout many of his letters. As believers, we have no reason to be anxious about anything, but we are to cast ALL of our cares and worries on the Lord, because He cares for us. To cast something to someone is like throwing a ball, but without the expecting to receive it back. To cast something is to trust the one who receives fully and recognize that it is no longer yours. This is what the Lord requires of those who follow Him wholeheartedly. Leave the driving to Him. Resist the temptation to get discouraged and frustrated when things do not go as well or as quickly as you hoped or expected they would. When you try to "drive" by controlling circumstances or outcomes, you acknowledge that you want to live for yourself. Frank Sinatra was famous for singing a song titled, "My Way." If you want to enjoy the peace of God that surpasses all understanding, you must die to selfish tendencies and relinquish the controls over every area of your life to the

One who gave you His life for those controls. Trust the Lord with ALL your heart, mind, strength, mouth, and money. He knows what is best for you. He is able to fulfill the work He began in you. Start today and give up the driver's seat and allow the Lord to direct your life in the way He wants it to go. Refuse to go it alone. This is the path taken by those who refuse to die to self. Let your day be covered with the confession, "Lord, not my will, but Yours be done in my life today." Learn daily how to turn the controls of your life over to the Lord by casting all the cares of this life on Him and serving Him without distractions. The cares and worries of this life distract us from what is most important: serving the Lord with an undivided heart. Fix your eyes on Jesus, the author and finisher of your faith, and trust Him to establish your thoughts. Remember, the greatest commandment is to love the Lord God with all our heart, soul, mind, and strength. We often exclude loving Him with our minds and allow thoughts of selfish ambition dominate our thinking, believing we can do it all by ourselves. This mindset is a great deception because it causes us to lean on our own understanding and become wise in our own eyes. Apart from Christ, there is no way to overcome the things that hinder us from becoming who God intended us to be. You and I must daily surrender our hearts, minds, and mouths to Him in order for our lives to move with His will.

According to the prophet Isaiah, the Lord's ways and thoughts are not like ours, nor is He like us. Too often, we miss God because we put Him on our level and think of Him on a human level points. Here what the Lord says, *"Seek the Lord while He may be found. Call upon Him while He is near. Let the wicked forsake His way,* [give up the controls] *And the unrighteous man his thoughts; Let Him return to the Lord,* [give Him the controls] ... *'For my thoughts are not your thoughts, Nor are your ways My ways,' says the Lord"* (Isaiah 55:6-8). Today is the day to change your way of doing things. Start seeking and calling on God by praying for His will to be done in your life and He will give you power to resist the temptation to take the controls back from Him. Stand firm on the belief that God is able to do what He said He would do for you. Don't allow the shine of self-made people seduce you into adopting the mindset that you are the controller of your destiny. You and I were created to live according to the plan devised by the one who created us to fulfill His purpose for our lives. No one was created to live for themselves. Relinquish the controls to the only One who knows the best journey for your life and leave the driving to Him. Rest in the assurance that His thoughts toward you are thoughts of peace and not evil, to give you a future and a hope.

VOWS

"When you make a vow to God, do not delay to pay it; For He has no pleasure in fools. Pay what you have vowed—Better not to vow than to vow and not pay." Ecclesiastes 5:4-5

During times of great suffering and life-threatening storms, we make promises out of desperation because we want immediate relief from our pain. We cry loudly and constantly until we receive what we want. How many times have you heard stories of people stranded at sea, lost in the forest, caught by an assailant, drowning in financial ruins, childless, jobless, homeless, spouseless, or without the means to survive? Our lives are filled with stories of loved ones who have cried out to us or God during difficult times. We have cried to someone whom we believed could help us. Many times, we have cried out to the Lord and promised to do whatever He said if He would only remove our difficulty. We have often added conditions to our prayers, in the hope of influencing the Lord to expedite our relief or grant us the desires of our hearts. We are sincere at the time, but fail to acknowledge our sinful natures. Jesus said that the spirit is willing but the flesh is weak. Yet we make vows to the Lord without pondering their long-term meaning or intending to follow through. After suffering the impact of a great storm and being in the belly of a hellish surrounding, Jonah remembered the Lord and said, "I will pay what I have vowed." It took profound isolation in the depths of the sea for Jonah to come to his senses and see that God does not take vows lightly. When we make promises to do Lord in our moments of painful desperation, we must remember that God expects us to fulfill them without hesitation or delay. In the law of Moses', this is what God said about vows, *"When you make a vow to the LORD your God, you shall not delay to pay it; for the Lord will surely require it of you and it would be sin to you. But if you abstain from vowing, it shall not be sin to you. That which has gone from your lips you shall keep and perform, for you voluntarily vowed to the LORD your God what you have promised with your mouth* (Deut. 23:21-23). The Lord took seriously the vows of the Israelites, and He takes ours seriously too.

Our society promotes vow breaking with continuous news of some celebrity couple divorcing. Marriage vows have become almost meaningless in today's world and it isn't much better in the American church. The excuse of "irreconcilable differences" is the number one reason for many divorces today. People are turning to matchmaking services or reality shows to find their "soul mates." What happened to the vow to love for better or worse, in sickness and health, for richer or for poorer, until death do us part? Where is the commitment to keeping vows that were voluntarily promised? If marriage vows have little value to the one who rashly and voluntarily made them, why would vows to an invisible God matter? The Lord our God takes no pleasure in those who use vows to flatter or manipulate for selfish gain. Vows are taken seriously by the Lord and this is why He would prefer we not make any promises to Him.

My blindness to the truth has been removed and now I see the error of my ways. When I was facing a difficult time in college, I asked for the Lord's intervention and help. I added the promise that I would study His Word like I studied for college if He would deliver me from my current troubles. He showed up with great power and relieved me from my problem. This was over thirty years ago, and I have partially fulfilled that vow, but not completely because I have filled my time with seeking monetary success. I have been reminded that my agreement with the Lord still stands and requires full payment, even if it takes the rest of my life. I can honestly say I have not fully devoted myself to the study of God's Word alone because of career opportunities that have consumed my time and energy. I have only done enough study to keep focused on God and faith and to prepare for speaking engagements, but I have not enrolled in a program in a formal institution or committed to independent study. I have access to numerous resources today in order to study thoroughly God's Word, that He may fulfill His plan for my life, but excuses keep distracting me. I am determined to make good on my promise and pay what I vowed to the Lord, which is being accomplished through this writing. I have chosen to take time out from fulfilling household and family chores and seek the Lord's Word on what He says about vows. I hope you will embrace Him with your time and renew the vows you made to Him when you were facing difficult times. What did you promise Him when you had no purpose, no direction, and no vision for your life? What did you promise Him when you were childless, jobless, homeless, spouseless, education-less, fatherless, family-less, health-less, helpless, or penniless? Pray and ask the Lord to remind you of any vows you have yet to fulfill. Proclaim the words of Jonah, "I will pay what I have vowed," for with the confession of the mouth a word is established; for by your words you will be justified or condemned.

HE IS ALWAYS HOLDING YOU!

"Listen to Me ... Who have been upheld by Me from birth, Who have been carried from the womb: Even to your old age, I am He, And even to gray hairs I will carry you! I have made, and I will bear; Even I will carry and will deliver you." Isaiah 46:3-4

When you face many afflictions and trials and feel pressed down on every side, know that you are being carried by your Father who is unseen. Be steadfast and unmovable in your faith in the Lord your God. Wait on Him until the storms pass over you and be fully persuaded that what He promised He is able to perform. If He loved you enough to inscribe your name in the palm of His hand, surely, He will lift you up and carry you on His wings, that you may overcome what seeks to sift your faith as wheat. He bore you and He will carry you when you put your trust in Him to be your strength in the midst of trouble. Know that many are the afflictions of the righteous, but the Lord delivers them out of them all, that His name may be glorified because they took refuge in Him. Those who wait upon the Lord are renewed with saving strength. Wait until the Lord lifts you up on His wings and carries you to the broad place He has prepared for you, a place in which your faith has come forth as gold. Never confess as the children of Israel did and say, "My way is hidden from the Lord," but know that the everlasting God, the Lord and Creator, is never faint or weak. He gives power to those who have no might and increases their strength because they chose to wait on Him. Hear what Isaiah said; "Those who wait on the Lord shall renew their strength; They shall mount up with wings like eagles, They shall run and not be weary, They shall walk and not grow faint" (Isaiah 40:31). Trust in the Lord to carry you through the storms of life and you will come out victorious. He will uphold you with His righteous right hand and strengthen you when you become weak, that you may say, "I am strong in Him." The message of the poem "Footprints in the Sand" is one of being carried by the Lord. Know that when you do not feel the presence of the Lord during difficult times, it is because He is carrying you.

Printed in the United States
By Bookmasters